THE SEARCH FOR
GOD AND
GUINNESS

A BIOGRAPHY OF THE BEER
THAT CHANGED THE WORLD

STEPHEN MANSFIELD

THOMAS NELSON
Since 1798

NASHVILLE   DALLAS   MEXICO CITY   RIO DE JANEIRO   BEIJING

Published in Nashville, Tennessee, by Thomas Nelson. Thomas Nelson is a registered trademark of Thomas Nelson, Inc.

Thomas Nelson, Inc., titles may be purchased in bulk for educational, business, fund-raising, or sales promotional use. For information, please e-mail SpecialMarkets@ThomasNelson.com.

Library of Congress Cataloging-in-Publication Data

Mansfield, Stephen, 1958-
  The search for God and Guinness : biography of a beer that changed the world / by Stephen Mansfield.
    p. cm.
  Includes bibliographical references.
  ISBN 978-1-59555-269-3
  1. Guinness (Firm)—History. 2. Beer industry—Ireland—History. 3. Brewing industry—Ireland—History. 4. Guinness family. I. Title.
  HD9397.I74G8575 2009
  338.7'99342—dc22

                                                          2009034023

Printed in the United States of America

11 12 13 14 QG 10 9 8 7 6

To Brian Wade:
Semper Fidelis

ALSO BY **STEPHEN MANSFIELD**:

Never Give In:
The Extraordinary Character of Winston Churchill

Then Darkness Fled:
The Liberating Wisdom of Booker T. Washington

Forgotten Founding Father:
The Heroic Legacy of George Whitefield

The Faith of George W. Bush

The Faith of the American Soldier

Benedict XVI: His Life and Mission

The Faith of Barack Obama

TABLE OF CONTENTS

PROLOGUE

I was sitting on a bench outside the Guinness Archives at the St. James's Gate Brewery in Dublin when I heard the question. It came from a blonde American teenager who sat with her boyfriend on the bench next to me.

"So, like, what does Guinness do?" she asked as the two conversed.

It was hard not to laugh. After all, at that very moment we were seated inside of a seven-story structure shaped like a glass of beer.

Still, the boyfriend was patient. "Well, baby," he said gently, trying to drain every sarcastic tone out of his voice, "they make beer. Lots of it. And they are known for it all over the world." You could tell he had answered questions like this before.

"But all kinds of people make beer," the blonde replied, her voice a slightly grating whine. "What's so big about *this* beer?"

Now at a loss, the boyfriend looked at me. Since I had an appointment at the Archives, I was wearing a sport coat and had a briefcase and must have looked like I could help. Besides, I was twice their age and for all they knew I worked for Guinness.

Turning to me with a pleading expression, the boyfriend said, "Sir, can you tell my girlfriend why Guinness is so famous?"

Now, I confess that my first impulse was to say, "No, and I doubt anyone could." But I knew this was just the irritation of the moment and, what is more, I remembered something I had just discussed with friends the night before: the Guinness story is largely unknown in the United States. Most of the books on the subject aren't available there and the story of the dark stout usually takes a back seat to the rise of American brewing empires like Busch and Coors. I realized these kids could hardly be blamed for not knowing the Guinness tale. So I gentled up.

"Yes, I can," I replied, and then I launched into a brief, informal survey of Arthur Guinness, his descendants, and the amazing thing that Guinness has become. But I kept the focus on the beer, and this, I quickly realized, was a mistake.

The two listened politely and then mumbled their thanks as they turned away. I knew I had not captured them. Refusing to let go of an audience, though, I said, "But what I think is really cool is how the Guinnesses used their wealth to help so many people." The couple immediately shifted back in my direction and said, "What do you mean?"

It was the kind of moment that a lover of the past lives for: two eager young faces and an interesting tale to tell. So I gave it my all. I told them how the Guinnesses were people of faith and how this faith moved them to do good in society. I recounted the deeds of Arthur Guinness—the righteous use of wealth and the Sunday schools and the antidueling association and his stand against extravagant living. I spoke also of the later generations and the high wages they paid their workers and the restoration of Ireland's historic landmarks and the huge gifts to build housing for the poor.

I was on a roll and the girl gestured to some of her friends who then turned off iPods and leaned in to hear. I could have kissed her.

Then I told them more of what I will tell you in this book, how a Guinness doctor surveyed the desperate needs of his day and asked the Guinness board to let him help. And I told them how one of the Guinness heirs took his new bride and moved into the slums to call attention to the blight of poverty in his land. And I told them how nothing they have read about Microsoft or Google compares with the way an Irish beer company cared for people when their grandparents were still young.

What a moment it was, with half a dozen American kids listening closely and nothing else in the world seeming to matter for those few minutes at St. James's Gate.

When I finished, the blonde girl stood up, her boyfriend in tow. "Well, then, let's go," she ordered. I chuckled a bit and, gently mocking her intensity, I asked, "So where are *you* going?" She half turned in my direction but spoke mainly to her friends as she said, "These people *did* something." Then, jabbing her finger fiercely toward the floor, she finished, "And I want to learn all about it."

Now, I am unbelievably sentimental about the young

Photo by Isaac Darnall

Author in the Guinness Storehouse archive room

and I could not let this go. "Yeah," I said, "go learn about them and then do something even bigger of your own."

I thought they might laugh me off, but I saw in their eyes a spark of gratitude that I thought they could have such possibilities in them. "Thank you," one of them said, and then I watched them drift into the next room, with all the flip-flops and bare midriffs and tattoos and piercings that mark their tribe.

And they seemed wonderful to me.

Just then, Eibhlin Roche, the Guinness archivist, stepped through her door: "Mr. Mansfield, are you ready to begin?"

Man, was I ever.

INTRODUCTION

This book was conceived in a myth, inspired by a weariness, and commissioned by a hope.

First, the myth.

It was a warm September Sunday morning when I joined a friend at his Presbyterian church and watched a black-robed minister mount his pulpit to begin the lesson for the day. What followed was a fine sermon, evidence both of the pastor's great learning and of his love for the people before him. Then, as he leaned into his conclusion, the pastor told a story. It was the tale of Arthur Guinness, founder of the famous brewing family, and of how in the mid-1700s he had walked the streets of Dublin pleading with God to do something about the drunkenness on the streets of Ireland. It seems that whiskey and gin were the rage in his day and the resulting devastation to his nation was more than young Arthur could stand. It was then, as he held this scourge of alcohol aloft in prayer, that Arthur heard his God speak: *Make a drink that men will drink that will be good for them.* And so, according to the learned Presbyterian parson, Guinness beer became God's answer for the moral blight of that time and all because Arthur Guinness was willing to listen and obey.

The sermon was a *tour de force*, yet when I heard the minister's tale of God and Arthur Guinness I knew it just wasn't true. It was a fiction spun from the precious few facts we know about the founder of the Guinness clan— and I knew as much because I had been studying the life of Arthur for quite some time.

In visiting with the minister after the service, I learned that he had come across the story on the Internet and was so touched by it that he decided to share it with his congregation as evidence that God can use mundane things for his purposes. And he can—and he has likely even used beer, as we shall see—but still the story isn't true. It is evidence of Mark Twain's insistence that a lie can run around the world before the truth can get its pants on, a maxim more true in an Internet age than at any time in history. Clearly, as this bit of misinformation makes its way from Web site to Web site, it is proof of our modern tendency to embellish the already miraculous, to help God out by putting a faster spin on his great works of old.

But this is to our generation's loss, for the truth of Arthur Guinness is as noble a tale and as much about devotion to God as anything the myth pretends. This genuine story is both thrilling and tender, too, even without dramatic myths about voices from heaven and beer brewed in answer to the moral crisis of an age. It is also inspiring, and all the more so because it involves, as the old creeds have said, God's use of "means," of secondary causes and what appear to be natural events. This makes the Guinness saga something of human scale, something we can relate to and emulate, while the myths merely conceal the truth through exaggeration and thus rob us of what we might gain from the story rightly told.

The fact is Arthur Guinness was indeed a great man of faith. Born on the estate of an archbishop and raised a loyal son of the Irish church, Arthur lived by the words that were his family motto: *Spes mea in deo* (My hope is in God). He was influenced by the revivalist John Wesley, who inspired him to use his wealth and talents to care for the hurting of mankind. Taking Scripture as his guide, Arthur did indeed serve the needy of his time and did indeed try to use his gifts in honor of his God.

Yet it is here that the story of Arthur is a departure from what the modern world is used to. We are used to preachers and to great noisy works for God. We are used to religion that is sometimes an escape from daily life and to faith as fixation on life in another world. What Arthur Guinness founded was a venture propelled by faith, yes—but by a kind of faith that inspires men to make their work in this world an offering to God, to understand craft and discipline, love of labor and skills transferred from father to son as sacred things. It was a venture of faith that took the fruit of the earth and, through study and strain, made of it something of greater value. Indeed, much of the great 250-year history of Guinness beer is a story in which wealth is gained through faith-inspired excellence and then used to serve others for the glory of God. This is what Arthur Guinness founded and this is the legacy Guinness beer still symbolizes to this day.

So as I shook that Presbyterian preacher's hand and made my way out into the September sun, I sensed that our age is poorer for not knowing the truth, for not having a chance to understand how the dramatic is not always evidence of the divine, and how the daily and the small are often how righteousness works its way through time. This is what the tale of Arthur Guinness and the generations that came after him had come to mean to me. And this is the story I started yearning to tell as I pondered the Arthur-myth and the damage done to a more noble truth.

Thus, the myth.

Now, the weariness.

In the months that led up to the presidential conventions of 2008, I had written a book called *The Faith of Barack*

Obama. It was less a labor of love for Obama, whom I admired but could not support, than it was an attempt to use his life to identify religious trends in American culture. So heated was that 2008 election and so religiously charged were the forces behind each man, Obama and McCain, that I found myself in the middle of a low-intensity civil war. My life was threatened. I was told I would surely rot in hell. Speeches were cancelled and friends even called to find out why I had decided to deny Christ. It was an angry, roiling season and it put me in a front-row seat to observe American politics at the time.

When it was all over, I found that I had grown weary—and not just from book tours and interviews. I was wearied by the emptiness of politics misplaced, politics as the meaning of life rather than as the art of protecting genuine life. I was fed up with mere party strife conducted like a war between gods. I yearned for the simple and the human, for the traditional and the rooted. I reveled in a favorite quote by G. K. Chesterton: "The most extraordinary thing in the world is an ordinary man and an ordinary woman and their ordinary children." And I longed to know the magic of the ordinary again.

It was then that I heard that Presbyterian sermon and I began to wonder what humanity and heritage and connection to real life might be found in the authentic Guinness story. When I began to read the books and I began to sit with the experts and then, in time, when I went to the brewery in Dublin, I started to understand.

I should be careful to say that it was not the Guinness of today that first captured my imagination, as shiny and high-tech and massive as it is. No, my historical imagination took flight and I could see this pure and beloved profession of brewing passing down through the successions of time. I could see barley and water and hops and yeast worked by masters into a drink that kept men from drunken insanity while it refreshed them and made them whole. I could see horses, well tended and loved, hauling casks of brew and I could see cask makers teaching their trade to clumsy young men. I could see ships on the seas carrying decks full of stout and I could see men on docks eagerly unloading what they hoped they would soon have a chance to taste. I could see workmen gathering after a day of sweat and lifting a glass of the national brew. And I could hear men at pubs laughing with relief at the day that was done and families raising a Guinness to toast the goodness of God in their lives.

I knew I had found it: that earthy, human, holy tale of a people honing a craft over time and of a family seeking to do good in the world as an offering to God. This was what my weary soul needed—a story thick like the smell of barley at the St. James's Gate Brewery and as filled with the bitter and the sweet as any generational tale is likely to be.

And so my weariness brought me to Guinness.

But so did my hope.

During the months in which I researched and wrote this book, the worst economic crisis since the Great Depression began unfolding. It started with an implosion of the housing market in the United States and spread to Wall Street, where predatory lending practices, unwise loans, and side bets on those loans—"swaps," they called them—exacerbated an already dire situation. Soon after, some of America's premier financial houses folded and most of those that survived did so only with federal aid.

It grew worse and greed seemed to permeate it all.

Suffocated by the gluttony and the grief that daily played themselves out on my office television, I turned with gratitude to the Guinness story. There I found an antidote—a drink from the spirit of an earlier age—that refreshed and gave me hope.

From the beginning of their corporate and family history, the Guinnesses had embraced their obligation to the needy of the world. This began at home, with their own employees. Edward Cecil Guinness, great-grandson of founder, Arthur, expressed a foundational company conviction when he said, "You cannot make money from people unless you are willing for people to make money from you." Accordingly, the Guinness brewery routinely paid wages that were 10 to 20 percent higher than average, had a reputation as the best place to work in Ireland, and, as important to many employees, allowed workers two pints a day of their famous dark stout.

Moreover, the benefits the company gave its employees surpass those even envisioned by modern companies like Google and Microsoft. Consider the snapshot provided by a Guinness company report in 1928, not an exceptionally enlightened time for corporate treatment of employees. Guinness workers at the brewery in Dublin enjoyed the attention of two fully qualified doctors who staffed an on-site clinic where any employee, wife, or child could receive treatment. These privileges extended to widows and pensioners, as well. The doctors were available night or day, made house calls, and would consult specialists on their patients' behalf if necessary.

There were also two dentists available to employees, two pharmacists, two nurses, a "lady visitor" who assured healthy conditions in workers' homes, and a masseuse. Hospital beds were provided both at the Guinness plant and at a "sanatoria" in the country, intended for patients recovering from tuberculosis.

This was only the beginning. Retirees received pensions "at the pleasure of the board," without having to make contributions of their own. This benefit extended to widows as well. If an employee or an employee's family member died, the company paid the majority of the funeral expenses.

To improve the lives of their employees, the company provided a savings bank on site and contributed to a fund from which workers could borrow to purchase houses. To make sure that life in these homes was all it could be, the company also sponsored competitions to encourage domestic skills, with cash awards for sewing, cooking, decorating, gardening, and hat making. Concerts and lectures were provided for the wives of workers, in the belief that the moral and intellectual level of a home would rise only to that of the mother or wife who lived there.

This same philosophy led to the company's sponsorship of guilds and associations of every kind. There was an association for the keeping and breeding of "Dogs, Poultry, Pigeons and Cage birds," for the cultivation of vegetables and flowers, and for the "encouragement of Home Industries." An athletic union was founded that sponsored competitions in Gaelic football, cricket, cycling, boxing, swimming, hurling, and tug-of-war. Beyond this, hardly a skill essential to brewing was not represented by a guild or professional development society, all sponsored by the company.

The educational benefits were also more generous than most modern corporations provide. Guinness paid for all its employees between the ages of fourteen and thirty to attend technical schools in Dublin and even funded more advanced education for those who were qualified. There was a lending library at the plant, a musical society, and "Workmen's Rooms"—which were lounges that allowed a hardworking man to read or just to think, to focus his mind on something beyond his labors. There were also classes in wood carving, cage making, fretwork, sketching, photography, cabinet making, handwriting, music, singing, and dancing.

The generosity of Guinness seemed unlimited. Every year, every employee was paid to take his family into the country for an "Excursion Day." Train fare was paid and money for food and entertainment was provided. Single men were allowed to take dates and, again, the company paid the bill. On the Jubilee of Queen Victoria, Guinness paid every employee an extra week's salary.

To immerse myself in this culture of generosity was a welcome respite from my own times, where greed and unwarranted privilege daily destroyed lives. It was not hard to see that the Guinness story might provide some balance, some tempering and grace, for our own hardened age. And so I was again drawn to the Guinness heritage for the lessons it might offer and for what it might mean for corporations trying to rise from the dust and build on a different model than the one that has led us so astray. This hope, that Guinness might teach us, guided my work—and lightened my heart.

It was a hope that held me fast to the Guinness tale.

And then there was the beer.

I confess that I came to the topic of beer much as an outsider. I had never been a beer drinker and did not consider myself any poorer for my choice. Still, the culture that surrounded beer and the fellowship that it seemed to inspire did attract me and I found myself looking in on the world of beer very much like a little boy with his face pressed against the window of the candy store.

This began, I imagine, in my youth when my father would come home at the end of the day. He was a U.S. Army officer and each afternoon he would walk into our house, tall and commanding in his uniform, and settle into his ritual of relaxation. His shirt was soon replaced by a sweater, his boots by his stocking feet. If he was in a playful mood, my brother or I would help him take off those boots and wrestling of some sort would usually ensue. Then, it was always the same: from the bedroom where he changed to the kitchen for supplies and then to the recliner to watch the evening news. And there was, too, the beer. Every evening it was a brew in a bottle or a glass and the handfuls of peanuts that my Georgia-bred soldier/father seemed unable to do without.

I recall watching him as he transformed from warrior to easy-going Dad. There was something about those moments alone with his newspaper and beer that seemed to me a liturgy, a mystery of manhood my father had mastered and that I hoped I would one day understand. It seemed to symbolize all the other moments in my father's life when beer played a role. Beer seems ever-present in military life and I had watched my parents drink it with friends at the officers' club and at battalion picnics and after rounds of golf. There was always the teasing and the laughter and the adult conversations that my young ears longed to understand and all of this was associated with the beer. Somehow I knew early on that the presence of beer changes human interaction, that it gentles the soul and brings about a less guarded state. My father was a different man when he drank a beer and not because he consumed very much of it—he never did—but rather because the beer seemed to give him permission to relax, to stand down and find a human connection to those nearby.

It was likely a passion to invade these mysteries that caused my friends in high school to give themselves to beer in excess. My family had been transferred to Des Moines, Iowa, by then and I was told by knowing friends in my new school that the most prized drink in the world was a concoction called Coors. But it was illegal in our state and so dozens of my friends had begun an underground railroad of beer from nearby states where Coors was legally sold. Our high school keggers and parties flowed thick with the stuff, but I confess that I never made peace with the taste of Coors, so I looked on, again, from without, more intrigued by the culture beer inspired in my father's world than by the drunken craziness my friends were determined to enjoy.

Decades passed. I went to college. I pastored. I wrote books. I lectured. I worked in politics. And I took stock of the state of friendship and bonding in my world. By this time home brewing had become a trend and brewery restaurants made an appearance in most every town. But something else had occurred. It was a cultural shift. Perhaps it was a product of the baby boomers growing older or it may have been the twentysomethings doing for beer and alcohol what their older brothers and sisters had done for coffee. Clearly, a beer with a friend—or the boss or the team or the spouse—had become very much the style.

At my local watering hole in Nashville, the Flying Saucer, this cultural shift was on grand display. I sat with my Diet Coke and watched church boards meet by the hour, each elder with beer in hand. I saw corporate staffers make presentations on notebook computers, interrupted only by a discussion of which beer of the 211 that the Flying Saucer serves would be featured in the second round. And then there were families trying out a Belgian brew and little old ladies giggling away as they ordered the pale ale of the day. Somehow, it seemed that we were trying to become European, that we no longer wrestled with the ethics of alcohol as in ages past but that we were desperate for those pleasant hours that a good beer and friends could sometimes mean.

This, too, endeared me to Guinness. I thought of the two and a half centuries of life lived with the dark stout in attendance at many a meaningful moment: when the baby was born or the grandfather died, when the son made it through school or the just-wed couple sheepishly locked the bedroom door. People naturally toast these changes with something in their glasses, something that they value and that brings them joy. For more than ten million people every day, that glass is full of Guinness. And their lives are certainly richer for what it can mean and for the friendship and fun they celebrate with those they hold dear.

And I confess, as an outsider to drinking and beer, I used to think it was all about the buzz, that drinking anything with alcohol was about escaping the present and drifting into a sloshy other world. But now I know something I did not before. Beer is not simply a means of drunkenness nor is it merely a lubricant to grease the skids to sin. Beer, well respected and rightly consumed, can be a gift of God. It is one of his mysteries, which it was his delight to conceal and the glory of kings to search out. And men enjoy it to mark their days and celebrate their moments and stand with their brothers in the face of what life brings.

So it was all of this—the unfortunate myth of Arthur, my weariness with politics at the center of life, my hope for a more noble corporate world and, yes, my curiosity at the fellowship of human beings and beer—that sent me on this journey. It is a search for heritage, faith, and craft. It is a hope for an impartation from generations past. It is a passion to understand the liturgies of men in concourse with one another.

It is the search for God and Guinness.

Photo by Isaac Darnall

SOME GUINNESS FACTS

- More than ten million glasses of Guinness are consumed each day worldwide. This is nearly two billion pints a year.

- In 1759, Arthur Guinness founded the Guinness brewery in Dublin by signing a lease for the famous property at St. James's Gate—a lease that gave him rights to that property for nine thousand years!

- Arthur Guinness founded the first Sunday schools in Ireland, fought against dueling, and chaired the board of a hospital for the poor.

- It is a myth that the water for brewing Guinness comes from the River Liffey. Most of the water comes from the streams of the Wicklow Mountains, which lie just south of Dublin.

- A Guinness worker during the 1920s enjoyed full medical and dental care, massage services, reading rooms, subsidized meals, a company-funded pension, subsidies for funeral expenses, educational benefits, sports facilities, free concerts, lectures and entertainment, and a guaranteed two pints of Guinness beer a day.

- During World War I, Guinness guaranteed all of its employees who served in uniform that their jobs would be waiting for them when they came home. Guinness also paid half salaries to the family of each man who served.

- In December of 1939, in the early days of World War II, Guinness gave every soldier serving in the British Army a pint of stout to enjoy with his Christmas dinner.

- A Guinness chief medical officer, Dr. John Lumsden, personally visited thousands of Dublin homes in 1900 and used what he learned to help the company fight disease, squalor, and ignorance. These efforts also led to the establishment of the Irish version of the Red Cross, for which Dr. Lumsden was knighted by King George V.

- The widget—the small plastic capsule that allows a can of Guinness to be properly nitrogenated—won the Queen's Award for Technological Achievement in 1991. In 2005, the British people voted it the greatest invention in the previous forty years.

- Guinness is now sold in 150 countries. It is brewed in 49 countries.

- In 2003, scientists at the University of Wisconsin reported that a pint of Guinness a day is good for the human heart.

- Henry Grattan Guinness, grandson of brewery founder Arthur Guinness, was a Christian leader of such impact that he was ranked with Dwight L. Moody and Charles Spurgeon in his day. He has been called the Billy Graham of the nineteenth century.

- Henry Guinness, who died in 1910, wrote best-selling books that not only predicted the end of Ottoman control of Jerusalem in 1917 but also the restoration of Israel in 1948.

- Guinness was known for its care of its employees. One Guinness family member who headed the brewery said, "You cannot make money from people unless you are willing for people to make money from you."

- In the 1890s, Rupert Guinness, future head of the brewery, received five million pounds from his father on his wedding day. Shortly after, he moved into a house in the slums and launched a series of programs that served the poor.

Photo by Isaac Darnall

BEFORE THERE
WAS GUINNESS

I t was William Shakespeare who wrote "what's past
is prologue," and I have always believed this is true,
but you would never have known it from the history
classes I was required to take in school. They seemed prologue to nothing. They had little connection to anything
that was to come, anything that might be relevant to the
meaning of real life. It was the "Age of This" and the "Era
of That." It was dates and dead people, all of it mind-
numbingly boring.

What makes all of those hours in history class worse in retrospect is how much I came to love history later. Like millions of other people in the world, if the surveys are true, I became enthralled with the past as an adult in a way I never could have with the dusty classroom version. History not only contained thrilling adventure from ages gone by, but also an explanation of my times and wisdom for life.

So when I went in search of the Guinness story, I took Shakespeare's maxim to heart and probed the history of beer prior to the beginning of Guinness in order to understand the world—and more specifically the world of beer—out of which the tale of Guinness grew. I have to tell you I was stunned. I have a doctorate in history and I have spent years studying the past in preparation for lectures and writing books, but never had I come across the huge role that beer has played through the centuries. So when I began searching for the story of beer in history, I was amazed to find not just a quiet little theme on the back lot of mainstream history, but a story that is woven through the great literature, civilizations, and movements of the human story.

Let me give you a small example of what I mean. Almost all of us are familiar with the story of the Pilgrims. Every Thanksgiving Americans at least allude to these forefathers and their *Mayflower* story and, certainly, it is a tale that holds a fascination all its own. But let me retell a portion of it here with a few completely accurate details added that you likely have not heard. You'll see what I mean when I say beer adds an interesting element to the retelling of the past, that it makes some of the great adventures of old even more endearing and unforgettable.

Consider this:

It was the foul New England winter of 1621 and the small band of Englishmen we call the Pilgrims were carving out a life on the barrens of Cape Cod. That they were alive at all was a miracle. Only months before, they had sailed for sixty-six days across a wild Atlantic Ocean that had tossed them about for weeks at a time. There had been deaths and days on end when they were locked in the 'tween deck for safety with screaming and crying and every kind of human waste floating in the bilge at their feet.

Now that they had put ashore, having signed the covenant declaring they ventured "for the Glory of God and the advancement of the Christian faith," their desperate situation was obvious to all. As their future governor, William Bradford, later wrote, "Being thus passed the vast ocean, and a sea of troubles before in their preparation, they had now no friends to welcome them nor inns to entertain or refresh their weatherbeaten bodies; no houses or much less towns to repair to, to seek for succour." They were alone on the edge of a wilderness, trying to complete their "errand into the wilderness" for God.

So in March of 1621, in this howling, frozen place, they worked to build their shelters against the cold. And they stood guard, for they had noticed the natives who watched at a distance. The Pilgrims had tried to approach them once, but this only frightened the nervous brown men away. The Pilgrims worked with muskets nearby, then, wary of the strange-looking men who gazed at them from the edge of the trees.

On March 16, a mercifully warmer day than in recent months, this standoff came to an end. Suddenly, a tall, muscular native strode out from the trees and began to approach. The Pilgrims quickly took their muskets in hand. They were startled, for the man coming toward them was an unsettling sight. He was nearly naked—"stark naked," they later said—with only a strand of leather about his waist and fringe about as wide as a man's hand covering his private parts. He carried a bow and two arrows and the Pilgrims noticed that his hair was long in the back but shaved at the front of his head. They had seen nothing like this back in England.

As startling as this Indian was to the Pilgrims, it was what happened next that shocked them most of all. The man neared, paused, and then shouted "Welcome!" in clear, perfect English. And then, more astonishing still, he asked—again, flawlessly in the Pilgrims' own tongue—if they had some beer.

Yes. Beer.

This is the truth, and you likely didn't know it because it is rarely mentioned in the textbooks or in the Thanksgiving specials on TV. It is right there, though, in *Mourt's Relation* and *Of Plymouth Plantation*, the two primary sources we have for the Pilgrim story. You see, this native's name was Samoset and as he told his story the Pilgrims learned that he had mastered their language while traveling with English ships up and down the coast of New England. He had grown fond of the Englishmen, had become accustomed to their ways, and had apparently developed a taste for English beer. Thus it was that Samoset and his quiet companion, Squanto, became part of the magnificent adventure these Pilgrims were destined to live.

And beer continued to play a defining role in the Pilgrim story. Consider, for example, how the Pilgrims came to decide to finally put ashore and start building their historic settlement.

When they first left the shores of England, the passengers of the *Mayflower* had plenty of beer for their voyage on board. This valuable supply was tended by the famous John Alden, hero of the Longfellow tale. But by the time they reached New England, their stores of beer were running desperately low. They saw this as threatening disaster. Beer for them was more than just an enjoyable drink. They not only believed that it had important medicinal qualities that they would need in the New World, but they, like most of the people of their time, drank beer for fear of drinking water. Since the teeming cities of Europe often polluted the nearby rivers and streams, deaths from drinking of these waters were not unknown, and seventeenth-century Europeans came to believe that most all water was unsafe. Beer, though, was seen as healthy and pure. We now know what people of that time did not: the boiling, which is part of brewing beer, and the alcohol that results kills the germs that sometimes contaminate water.

It was fear of running out of beer, then, that partially forced the Pilgrims to leave the *Mayflower* and get busy building their new lives on shore. They had reached the New World in late November but had spent nearly a month looking for a good site on which to build. As William Bradford later wrote of those nervous, searching days, "We had yet some beer, butter, flesh and other victuals left, which would quickly be all gone and then we should have nothing to comfort us." Finally, just when their supplies had nearly run out, they thought they spied some good land for a settlement. Of this Bradford wrote, "So in the morning, after we had called on God for direction, we came to this resolution—to go presently ashore again and to take a better view of two places which we thought most fitting for us; for we could not now take much time for further search or consideration, our victuals being much spent, especially our beer." Thus was Plymouth, Massachusetts, founded.

It is testimony to the importance of beer in their story that the brewery was the first permanent building the Pilgrims constructed. As Gregg Smith has written in his excellent history of beer, "Their critical shortage made a brewhouse a priority among the structures built that first winter in Plymouth. Even if the Pilgrims' supply weren't scarce, the need for a brewery was immediate. The population of the small colony expanded faster than ale could be shipped from Europe. And of all the hardships the settlers endured, the lack of beer caused them the most displeasure."

To prevent a similar experience, when the Puritans sailed to New England a decade later in 1630, they made sure that beer was in plentiful supply. Just one of their five ships, the *Arbella*, carried 42 tuns of beer. Since a tun was 252 gallons, this meant that at least 10,000 gallons of beer refreshed the Puritans on their journey to the New World. And, again, a brewhouse proved a priority when they began building their new city called Boston.

Now, my point in all of this is not that beer captures everything that is important in the Pilgrim adventure or in the later Puritan settlement in the New World. Of course not. But it was there, nonetheless—beloved and needed by the people of that day, and it was such a priority that it shaped many of the decisions that these forefathers made. In other words, it was often a motive force, a reason that people did what they did, and not just because it gave pleasure but also because it was a source of the health and the nourishment and the purity that our ancestors needed at the time.

This is very much as it was all throughout human history. Beer helped to shape entire civilizations and often conditioned the critical decisions they made. In fact, if one professor is correct, beer may have been the reason man became civilized in the first place. So let's take a moment to correct the grand omission of beer from the story of the past, and consider for a while the role beer has had to play.

This bit of beer heritage will prepare us well for exploring the later glories of Guinness.

Though you might not suspect it if you walk through the gleaming stainless steel canyons of a modern brewery, the brewing of beer can be a relatively simple affair. A grain, usually barley, is wetted to allow it to germinate or, more simply, to sprout. When it does, it is quickly dried. It has thus been *malted*. This malted barley is then roasted. How long it is roasted will determine the color of the beer it produces, a process that is obviously important in brewing a

Roasted barley in the Guinness Storehouse

dark beer like Guinness. This malt is *mashed,* which means that it is soaked long enough in water to allow the process that converts the natural starches of the malt into the sugars that are necessary for fermentation. More water is then added to this mash, essentially to wash the sugars off of the grains and into a thick, sweet liquid called *wort.* This wort is boiled, and afterward the dried flowers from the hops vines are usually added for flavor, though throughout history the flavor of beer has been enhanced by nearly every kind of fruit, spice, or honey known to man.

After this hopped wort is cooled, yeast is added. A brewer once told me that he thinks of yeast as a bunch of frat boys invading the party of brewing. They rush into the mix and spend their time eating, passing gas, and reproducing. What come of this is the alcohol and carbon dioxide make that sweet, hop-tasting water called wort into beer.

This is the way beer is made and knowing this helps us to imagine how beer came about in those first uncertain ages of human history. The truth is it was probably a wonderful accident, but to understand how this might be so, we have to know a little bit about the beginnings of mankind.

Our first ancestors, the men and women who existed at the very dawn of time, probably lived in the Fertile Crescent region of the world, an arch of land that stretches from modern Egypt up the Mediterranean coast and after touching the southeast corner of Turkey drops down again through the border between Iraq and Iran. The region is aptly named, for particularly in early history its soil was luxuriant and rich, its vast, fruitful regions teeming with game. It was an ideal environment for nearly every kind of life—and particularly for dense strands of wild wheat and barley.

If the theories of historians are right—and God knows, they often aren't—the region was at first home to roving bands of hunter-gatherers who would have hunted the abundant wild game and gathered the edible cereal grains that grew so profusely. Over time, these nomadic men would have learned how to bake these widely available grains into bread and this, we are told, led almost directly to the discovery of beer.

Again, this discovery probably happened in a series of accidents. Early men would have learned not only how to harvest barley but also how to create earthen jars to store it. It is not hard to imagine that at some point someone might have left this stored barley exposed to rain. Of course, soaking barley starts the malting process. We can picture our disgusted early ancestor—let's call her Nonna—waking up to the soaked mess that once was the proud product of her hours of backbreaking work. She would have decided to do something to rescue this valuable grain. Being boldly experimental and desperately frugal, Nonna tried to dry the grain by spreading it out under the sun. Malted barley would have been the result. Then, when Nonna baked this barley into bread, her family might have commented that the bread was much sweeter than anything she had served before.

Now, if Nonna's crudely malted barley, wetted by the rain and dried under the sun, was exposed to the rain again, the result would have been very much like wort: the natural starches of malt being converted to sugar and dissolved in water. Then, when Nonna left her jars of this sweet grainy mixture open, natural airborne yeast would have begun its work, and in time Nonna's jars would have been filled with a foamy, bubbly substance. She would have tasted it, shared it with her friends, and eventually all would have agreed that this tasty, lightly intoxicating liquid had to be made again. Curiosity, experimentation, and pleasure would have played a role through the centuries and this would have eventually given us some time-honored methods for brewing a primitive beer.

There is a professor at the University of Pennsylvania named Solomon Katz who believes that not only did beer evolve in exactly this way, but that the discovery of beer may have been why early man stopped his hunter-gatherer ways and began to build cities. "My argument," Dr. Katz has said, "is that the initial discovery of a stable way to produce alcohol provided enormous motivation for continuing to go out and collect these seeds and try to get them to do better." He means that rather than early men relying on wild stands of barley to make brew, they would have begun growing the barley themselves in hopes of producing a better yield. And this attachment to their fields of barley would have caused them to settle in one place, to begin living in larger communities, and to eventually evolving the cities from which civilization gets its name. The word *civilization* literally means "living in cities." Thus,

Dr. Katz believes that beer may have been a primary reason man moved from the wild into cities and began building the great civilizations of the ancient world.

He is not the first. The ancient Sumerians would have agreed with Dr. Katz. In Sumer, the region at the head of the Persian Gulf where human history began (largely because writing emerged there around 3400 BC), this connection between beer and civilization was not a theory but a celebrated certainty. In fact, this role of beer in the making of civilization was put into poetic form in the world's first great literary work, known today as *The Epic of Gilgamesh*. Now, like me, you probably remember something about this from school, but we certainly don't recall that it had anything to do with beer. Apparently, though, it did. It seems that Gilgamesh was a Sumerian king who ruled around 2700 BC and whose life inspired myriad myths, beloved not only by the Sumerians but also by the Akkadians and the Babylonians. The *Epic* is the tale of Gilgamesh's adventures with his friend Enkidu, a wild man who, not unlike mankind itself, begins life running naked in the wilderness. In time, he is taught the ways of civilization by a young woman who takes him to a shepherds' village so he can learn the first stages of civilized life.

They placed food in front of him,
they placed beer in front of him;
Enkidu knew nothing about eating bread for food,
and of drinking beer he had not been taught,

The young woman spoke to Enkidu saying:
"Eat the food, Enkidu, it is the way one lives.
Drink the beer, as is the custom of the land."
Enkidu ate the food until he was sated,
He drank the beer—seven jugs!—and became
    expansive
and sang with joy.
He was elated and his face glowed.
He splashed his shaggy body with water,
and rubbed himself with oil, and turned into a
    human.

Obviously, the Sumerians not only believed that beer helped make civilization but that it was also part of what

Hops Vines

made a civilized man. They probably believed this because Dr. Katz is right: beer is part of what moved men to stop their hunter-gatherer ways and to build cities, thus, again, leading to the great city-states of early human history.

This may seem extreme, but it makes more sense when we reclaim another truth they forgot to tell us in history class: beer was regarded as sacred in the ancient world. Frankly, I don't find this hard to imagine. The making of beer must have seemed to the ancients, much as it sometimes does today, like a miracle. To a pagan mind-set, it must have seemed a gift of the many gods. In a Jewish and later Christian worldview, it was a blessing of the one God's creation. To all, the brewing of beer must certainly have seemed like a sacred cooperation with the mysteries of the universe. A brewer once told me that he did not think of himself as brewing beer, but rather as creating the conditions in which brewing takes place. He wets the barley and then stands back. It germinates. He dries it, roasts it, and adds water. Again he stands back as starch converts to sugar. He washes this sugar-coated grain, boils what results, adds hops and then waits while yeast makes his hoppy sugar water into beer. He told me he felt closer to God brewing beer than he did in church, because when he is brewing he feels like he is participating in the secret ways of the Creator.

This is what the ancient Sumerians felt too—a religious awe of beer. They were so captured by the holiness of brewing that they decided the sacred craft should be practiced only in temples. This decision in turn shaped many of their myths and their understanding of the gods, most of which had some connection to beer. For example, the oldest recipe for beer known to man is found in the poem "The Hymn to Ninkasi," an ode to the Sumerian goddess who lived on mythical Mount Sabu—"the mountain of the tavern keeper."

The Babylonians, always willing to copy from other cultures, absorbed this Sumerian theology of beer. Their word for beer, *kassi*, was taken directly from the name of the Sumerian goddess Ninkasi, though they took this convergence of beer and religion beyond anything the Sumerians ever imagined. For the Babylonians, beer was the chief offering to the gods. Each god expected its own special brew, and an army of priests made sure that every ounce of sacrificial beer was brewed in the proper way. The Babylonians were so concerned with correct brewing for fear of their gods that they gave human history its first laws governing the production of beer—some of which sentenced clumsy brewers to death.

At about the same time that Sumerian and Babylonian cultures were elevating beer to religious heights, the Nubians just south of Egypt were engaged in a flourishing beer culture as well. This is important not only because it proves that beer was probably discovered in a number of places simultaneously, but because it also confirms that Africans had an early and native skill for brewing beer—a skill that is certainly in evidence in the region to this day.

The Nubians were exceptionally skilled at brewing beer and it is likely that their word for beer, *bousa*, is where we get our modern word *booze*. They not only brewed a standard beer (called *hktsty*), but also a spiced beer called *hes* or *hek* that was among the first of its kind.

Of all the ancient peoples, though, it was the Egyptians who most put beer at the heart of their religious worldview. We can see this clearly in the myth they used to explain the origins of beer. Apparently Osiris, the god of agriculture and lord of the afterlife, made a mixture of water and sprouted grain but then forgot about it and left it in the sun. He returned to find that his gruel had fermented. He drank it and was so pleased that he made it one of his blessings to mankind. Now, we read this story and realize that it parallels the human discovery of beer almost exactly. But this is very much what ancient myths were—human experience writ large—and they give us insight into how the ancient world thought about life and beer.

No culture wove beer into religion like the Egyptians. Beer was consumed as part of temple rituals and offered to the gods as sacrifice. There were gods for every stage of the brewing process and sometimes it is difficult to keep these gods apart. Though Osiris is said to have discovered beer, the Egyptians believed that Isis, the deity of nature, first gave beer to mankind. And, Hathor, the goddess of joy, is supposed to have invented all the processes of brewing. Then there is Menqet, whose inscription at the temple of Dendra proclaims her as "the goddess who makes beer."

There simply is no end to it all. Beer was so revered as a holy substance that a god was necessary for every human act connected to it, from the growing of grain to the final ceremonial act of consumption.

In fact, one Egyptian myth actually credits beer with saving all mankind—and this gives us some insight into how important beer was in the Egyptian world. It seems Ra, the sun god, came to believe mankind was plotting against him. He dispatched the goddess Hathor to punish his human enemies, but later Ra remembered how fierce Hathor's wrath could be and took pity on mankind. He decided to brew a huge amount of beer—some seven thousand jars of it—and then he dyed it red and spread it over vast fields, where it reflected like a mirror. Hathor passed by on her bloody mission, stopped to admire her reflection, and then stooped down to drink some of the beer. The goddess became so intoxicated that she forgot about her assignment and mankind was spared.

Their mythology aside, the Egyptians also made one of the most important early contributions to beer history: they are the first culture to have explored the health benefits of brewed drink. In what amounts to the *Physicians' Desk Reference* of ancient Egypt, there are over seven hundred different prescriptions that mention beer as a medicine in the Ebers Papyrus. So essential was the drink to health and well-being in the Egyptian view that barley brew is mentioned as early as 3000 BC in the *Book of the Dead* as a necessity for the journey into the afterlife. This explains why archaeologists almost always discover beer vats in the tombs of Egyptian pharaohs.

It is an interesting side note that most of the beer drinking I have described so far was done not from a glass but rather from a big vat and through a reed, a primitive version of the straw. Cups and glasses were developed later in history than you might think, and so when men drank beer in early centuries they usually pushed a reed down into a communal vat of beer. This was necessary in part because brewing was not as refined as it later became and beer always had a thick layer of grain mash floating on the top. To drink the good brew from below this unsightly and smelly mess, the ancients used reeds. This is confirmed by the fact that one of the first depictions of beer drinking we have is from a seal found at Tepe Gawra in Mesopotamia that dates from around 4000 BC. It shows two figures drinking with very long reeds from a vat that rises approximately to their shoulders. The vat is so tall that the two figures have to stand to drink. This seems to have been the Egyptian custom for quite some time. As late as 434 BC, Xenophon, the Greek historian, wrote of this way of drinking beer in his *Anabasis*: "For drink, there was beer which was very strong when not mingled with water, but was agreeable to those who were used to it. They drank this with a reed, out of the vessel that held the beer, upon which they saw the barley swim."

This Egyptian fascination with beer is important to us now because it came to shape the whole course of western brewing history. The Roman historian Pliny the Younger, who lived from AD 61 to 112, wrote extensively of how the Egyptians taught brewing to the Greeks, and how they in turn gave this knowledge to the Roman world. Greeks are usually associated in history with wine, but they had an interest in beer as an expression of culture, as a source of health, and, of course, for the pure enjoyment. The Greek historian Herodotus wrote a detailed treatise on beer in 460 BC and Sophocles, the father of theater, lectured widely on the value of daily beer as part of a healthy life. This love of beer and the skills of brewing that the Greeks captured from the Egyptians took root in the eager soil of the Roman Empire and was thus passed on as a gift to the ongoing course of western civilization. Pliny estimated that by the first century there were more than two hundred types of beer being brewed in Europe. Part of this passion for brew came from the Roman belief that beer gave strength and energy. Soldiers drank it before battle and athletes consumed it by the gallon. This may explain why the Latin word for beer is *cerevisium*, which means "strength."

Since our story is going to eventually take us to the Ireland of Arthur Guinness, it is important for us to know that the brewing of beer existed in the British Isles long before Roman times. It may have been discovered there much as it was in the other regions we've surveyed, in the same instantaneous and independent manner. In the first century, Pedanius Dioscorides, a Greek pharmacologist, traveled extensively throughout the Roman Empire searching for new substances with medicinal qualities. As he traveled among the Britons and the Hiberni—the Roman name for the Irish—he recorded that they produced an ale made from barley. It was called variously *cuirim*, *courm*, or *courmi*, and it is even mentioned in the first-century Irish saga *The Cattle Raid of Cooley*, the central tale in the Irish mythology known as the Ulster Cycle. One of the great Irish legends, it describes the Irish king Conchobar mac Nessa drinking this cuirim "until he falls asleep therefrom."

I find it interesting, given the controversies over alcohol that would eventually erupt in the history of the Christian church, that the arrival of Christianity in the world and its eventual sway over the empire did not diminish the Roman love of beer. For the early Christians, drunkenness was the sin—as their apostles had repeatedly taught—and not the consumption of alcohol. After all, their Lord had miraculously created wine at a wedding feast, the fledgling church drank wine at its sacred meals, and Christian leaders even instructed their disciples to take wine as a cure for ailments. Clearly, beer and wine used in moderation were welcomed by the early Christians and were taken as a matter of course. It was excess and drunkenness and the immorality that came from both that the Christians opposed. Many historians have noted that this positive Christian perspective on alcohol probably even encouraged brewing, because it both sanctioned a temperate love of beer and welcomed beer as an alternative to more high-alcohol drinks. This theory is supported by the fact that beer is so intertwined with the history of the Christian faith that it is tempting to believe that Christians discovered it. Perhaps in its holy and moderate use, they did.

As Christians captured the Roman world with their ideals and then took their gospel to non-Roman lands, beer was very much a part of the story. For example, around the turn of the fifth century, the revered St. Patrick introduced the Christian gospel to the wild and pagan land of Ireland. Always at his side was Mescan, the great saint's personal brewmaster. It seems that Patrick understood godly hospitality and captured many an Irish tribal chieftain with his tasty beer before he won the man for God. In other words, yes, beer played a role in the winning of Ireland for Christ. Beer also played a role in the miracles the great saint performed. According to legend, Patrick was once dining with the King of Tara when "The wizard Lucatmael put a drop of poison into Patrick's cruse (an old English word for *pitcher*), and gave it into Patrick's hand: But Patrick blessed the cruse and inverted the vessel, and the poison fell thereout, and not even a little of the ale fell. And Patrick afterward drank the ale."

Some sense of the importance of beer to medieval Christians is indicated by the many patron saints of beer celebrated by the Catholic church. Chief of these is St. Arnou, or Arnold, who once said, "From man's sweat and God's love, beer came into the world." Yet the miracle that led to his canonization happened after his death. When he passed from this life in AD 640, the people of his hometown went to retrieve his body from the monastery where he had retired. As his friends carried Arnou's body the weary distance home, they stopped in the village of Champigneulles, where they hoped to have a glass of beer. However, in the entire village only one mugful of beer could be found. They decided to pass the mug around for every man to at least have a sip. Amazingly, each man was able to drink his fill and the beer never ran out. The people came to believe that Arnou had performed this wonder from beyond the grave and thus the church made him the patron saint of beer.

There were other saints associated with beer, of course. St. Bartholomew was the patron saint of mead drinkers, or those who drank beer fermented from honey. St. Brigid was the famous Irish saint who labored in a leper colony and once asked God to turn bathwater into beer so that her lepers could also enjoy the taste of brew. According to the Catholic church, God did and so Brigid was made a saint. And then there was St. Columbanus. He once came upon a gathering of pagans who were about to sacrifice a keg of beer to the idol of their god. Their plan was to offer the keg on a sacred fire, but Columbanus began to preach and it wasn't long before the idol was burned instead. Afterward, Columbanus told the pagans that beer must always be received with thanksgiving to the true God before it can be rightly consumed. All of these became saints and all of their stories became part of the medieval worldview.

Beer was also in attendance at the birth of the Holy Roman Empire and this was largely because the emperor

Charlemagne loved beer and insisted on raising its quality throughout his domains. While conquering most of Europe and revitalizing art, religion, and culture as he went, he elevated the position of brewers in the empire, supported innovations in brewing science, and even formed a kind of brewing think tank to give him advice. His chief brewer was a man known to history as St. Gall, who came to Charlemagne fresh from his ministry among beer-loving Celts. St. Gall brought many Celtic ideas to his brewing endeavors and ended up enhancing nearly every stage of the brewing process. Charlemagne's reforms—and the eager work of monasteries throughout the Christian world—gradually made the church the primary brewer and wholesaler of beer in society. Men quickly learned that being in right relationship with the local religious leaders guaranteed access to beer. Soon the beer served at religious functions became known as "church ale," and this gave rise to a number of new terms, including *bridal*, originally the term "bride ale," the beer new brides served to those who gave them wedding gifts.

Charlemagne's support for brewing enhanced an already vibrant Christian beer culture in the medieval church, one that is difficult to exaggerate. An example comes to us from a letter that Pope Gregory wrote to Archbishop Nidrosiensi of Iceland. In it, Gregory describes how some children in the medieval period were baptized not with holy water but with beer. This was likely because beer was cleaner than water and for the baptizing priest it was also in more convenient supply. Still, the reference has become a symbol of how much the church of the time was almost literally immersed in beer.

The rise of monastic orders only strengthened this religious attachment to beer. Monasteries brewed beer as a social service—because it was a healthier drink than water and with less alcohol than the harder liquors a man might choose—but also to raise the funds that a monastic enterprise required. Naturally, the beer drinking of the monks themselves often became the subject of a laugh or two, as one ditty from the period reveals.

> To drink like a Capuchin is to drink poorly;
> To drink like a Benedictine is to drink deeply;
> To drink like a Dominican is pot after pot;
> But to drink like a Franciscan is
> to drink the cellar dry.

Though the church certainly maintained a monopoly in the beer trade, other sources soon emerged. Peasant wives had long brewed beer at home for their families and the servants in castle kitchens brewed for their masters in much the same way. This was nothing new. Yet by the end of the twelfth century, other masters of the brewing trade were slowly emerging. Taverns and inns began springing up in towns and along major roads, and many of these also brewed their own beer. These early brewpubs sometimes transformed into commercial breweries, some of which survive to this day—and more than a few of which were managed by female brewers, called *brewsters*, who were quickly becoming common throughout Northern Europe.

An explosion of such brewpubs and taverns came on the heels of one of the worst disasters to befall the western world. In 1347, a nearly invisible creature—*Yersinia pestis*—likely embedded itself in a rat, which in turn boarded a banana boat bound for Northern Europe from the Crimea. The result was the Black Plague, which led to four years of terror and more than forty million agonized deaths. It was an age of suffering, and though it may seem heartless to discuss it, the impact on beer and brewing in the years afterward was nothing less than astonishing. In the years following the plague, a dramatically smaller population shared the wealth of Europe, which still thrived much as it had prior to the years of death. By 1400, the average worker made twice the wages he might have made for the same work only one hundred years before. This meant more disposable income and time to travel, all of which fed the already thriving trade of brewing beer.

With wealth on the rise and travel the fashion, markets and fairs sprang up throughout Europe. In their wake came taverns and inns, brewpubs and breweries. In lower England alone, the number of drinking establishments grew from nearly none in 1300 to more than seventeen thousand by the year 1577. This meant a rate of increase of one new tavern a week. During this same period, London boasted a population of some thirty-five thousand residents within its city limits, yet it also contained more than 354 taverns and another 1,330 brewshops—one alehouse or tavern for every twenty-one people. And in Dublin, the city that would one day be home to Arthur Guinness, a survey published in 1610 estimated that there were more than 1,100 alehouses and nearly one hundred breweries and brewpubs—and this in a town of only four thousand families!

This dramatic increase in the number of sources for beer began raising concerns about standards of quality in brewing. These concerns were so widespread that when the English barons met King John at Runnymede to insist on the Magna Carta, one of their demands was for uniform brewing standards. It is no wonder. The beer of the day was a far cry from what we think of as beer now. Because yeast was unknown, the fermentation process occurred naturally through airborne yeast and was often incomplete. Beer was flat and very low in alcohol as a result. To compensate, brewers flavored it with spices. Sometimes even peppers were used. The description that comes to us from the 1200s portraying English beer as "muddy, foddy, fulsome, puddle, stinking" seems apt. A famous rhyme cited by Andrew Boorde in 1540 expresses the same sentiment.

> Ich am a Cornishmann, ale I can brew
> It will make one to cacke, also to spew
> It is thick and smokey and also it is thin
> It is like wash as pigs had wrestled there in.

As the number of breweries in Europe continued to rise, Germany took the lead in regulating brewing to improve quality. In 1487, Duke Albert IV issued a set of regulations that became the basis for the *Reinheitsgebot* of 1516. Best translated as "purity order," the *Reinheitsgebot* was called the German Beer Purity Law in English and was famous for defining the ingredients of beer as water, barley, and hops. The inclusion of yeast would have to wait until the 1800s, when Louis Pasteur explained to the world the role of microorganisms in fermentation. The *Reinheitsgebot* did indeed improve the quality of German beer; so much so that many brewers in Germany claim to abide by the standards to this day. These German innovations had no effect in England, though, which so reacted to the idea of using hops in beer that it banned the practice as a contamination. It was a view that prevailed well past 1524, when widespread English complaint took the form of this popular rhyme.

Hops, Reformation, Bays, and Beer
Came to England in one bad year.

The *Reinheitsgebot* helped make German beer among the best in the world. Unfortunately, it did so just prior to the Reformation, which had the twin effect of both celebrating beer more than any movement in church history and serving to close the very monasteries that brewed most of the world's beer at the time. Martin Luther could not have anticipated this result when he nailed his Ninety-five Theses to the Wittenberg Church door in 1517. His goal was to reform the Roman Catholic Church, not break from it. Yet when the church authorities stood firm and tried to destroy the fledgling Protestant movement, they only succeeded in fanning the flames of the revolt. As Reformation ideas captured hearts and minds throughout Europe, priests and nuns renounced their vows, Roman Catholic cathedrals became Protestant churches, and monasteries closed, thus decreasing the production of beer. While this decline in brewing would not have deterred Martin Luther from his reforming work, he certainly would have grieved the loss of any fine brew, for he was among the great beer lovers of Christian history.

Historians Will and Ariel Durant have written in *The Story of Civilization: The Reformation* that at the time of Luther, "a gallon of beer per day was the usual allowance per person, even for nuns." This may help to explain why beer figures so prominently in the life and writings of the great reformer. He was German, after all, and he lived at a time when beer was the European drink of choice. Moreover, having been freed from what he considered to be a narrow and life-draining religious legalism, he stepped into the world ready to enjoy its pleasures to the glory of God. For Luther, beer flowed best in a vibrant Christian life.

It is important to know that Luther's hometown of Wittenberg was a brewing center, that his wife, Katie, was a skilled brewer at her convent before she left it to marry him, and that in his day every occasion of life from weddings to banking was graced by the presence of beer. This was only good news to Luther. Inviting a friend to his wedding, he once wrote, "I am to be married on Thursday . . . Katie and I invite you to send a barrel of the best Torgau beer, and if it is not good, you will have to drink it all yourself!" This is typical of his playfulness, his boldness, and his passion for good German beer.

Having wrestled his soul out of its harsh theological constraints, Luther tried to understand the world afresh in a consistently biblical light. He reexamined, reapplied, and, where necessary, reformed according to a fiery biblical worldview. And he spared no one, from the pope to nuns and priests, from extremist Protestants to those who wouldn't live life fully in the love and grandeur of God. He did not suffer fools lightly and could barely stand those who feared moral excess and so retreated from everything that might tempt them in the world. "Do not suppose that abuses are eliminated by destroying the object which is abused," he once wrote. "Men can go wrong with wine and women. Shall we then prohibit and abolish women?"

Luther spent much of his life in the taverns of Wittenberg and not just because he loved to drink beer. He often mentored his students there, studied there, met important visitors there, and, upon occasion, even taught classes there. The time he spent in taverns and inns gave him a chance to look out onto the world as it was in his day, to experience and to observe. He surely chatted with prostitutes, helped carry drunks out the fair door, and may have mediated more than his fair share of spats between tipsy husbands and wives. The tavern was where Luther learned of the world he was called to reform with the gospel of Christ.

These hours of learning from life around beer must have led him to his famous definition of intoxication. "Drunkenness," he wrote, is "when the tongue walks on stilts and reason goes forward under half a sail." This definition posed no challenge to Luther, though, for he is never described as drinking to excess. Instead, he viewed drink as good for the body, an aid to social life, and a gift of God. "If God can forgive me for having crucified Him with Masses twenty years running," Luther once boomed, "He can also bear with me for occasionally taking a good drink to honor Him."

John Calvin, Luther's fellow reformer, felt very much

iStock Photos

Martin Luther

the same way, though this is contrary to the image of him that has come to us through time. Perhaps we should have known better. In his famous *Institutes of the Christian Religion*, Calvin wrote, "We are nowhere forbidden to laugh, or to be satisfied with food . . . or to be delighted with music, or to drink wine." The great Genevan reformer also wrote, "It is permissible to use wine not only for necessity, but also to make us merry."

Like Luther, Calvin worked hard to hammer out a consistently biblical worldview. He wanted all of his life to be submitted to the rulership of Jesus Christ and yet he did not want to miss some grace or provision of God because of flawed theology or religious excess. He and Luther had seen too much of that in their pre-Protestant lives. "The use of gifts of God cannot be wrong, if they are directed to the same purpose for which the Creator himself has created and destined them," he insisted. In his little classic, *The Golden Booklet of the True Christian Life*, Calvin developed the case that God has "made the earthly blessings for our benefit, and not for our harm":

> If we study . . . why he has created the various kinds of food, we shall find that it was his intention not only to provide for our needs, but likewise for our pleasure and for our delight . . . . For, if this were not true, the Psalmist would not enumerate among the divine blessings "the wine that makes glad the heart of man, and the oil that makes his face to shine."

This robust Reformation theology, which taught enjoying God's creation and doing all that is not sinful to the glory of God, filtered into the centuries that followed the reformer's work. This likely comes as a surprise to those who confuse biblical Christianity with the antisaloon leagues and prohibitionism of later history. The truth is that most post-Reformation Christians believed as their first-century fathers did—that drunkenness is sin but that alcohol in moderation is one of the great gifts of God.

Thus, John Wesley drank wine, was something of an ale expert, and often made sure that his Methodist preachers were paid in one of the vital currencies of the day—rum. His brother, Charles Wesley, was known for the fine port, Madeira, and sherry he often served in his home; the journals of George Whitefield are filled with references to his enjoyment of alcohol. At the end of one of his letters, he wrote, "Give my thanks to that friendly brewer for the keg of rum he sent us," and in another, "I believe God will take Georgia into his own hands. Its affairs have lately been before the House of Commons," where, thankfully, "the use of rum was granted." The revered colonial American pastor and theologian Jonathan Edwards viewed alcohol in much the same way. According to biographer Elizabeth D. Dodds, Edwards grew up in the home of a father who "turned out a locally famed hard cider in the orchard behind his house." Though he was not known to drink much at a time, Edwards was famous among his friends for nursing a glass of punch throughout an evening with family or while preparing his sermons at night.

Clearly, then, though the Reformation diminished the production of beer temporarily by closing many of the European monasteries where beer was brewed, it also served the cause of beer and alcohol well by declaring them gifts of God and calling for their use in moderation. This, in time, led to a restoration of beer brewing and even gave it a noble purpose—offering beer to the world as an alternative to the hard liquor that so often meant destruction in human lives.

Now I confess that when I started the research for this book, I knew very little of what you have read in this chapter. None of my academic courses or reading prepared me for the significant role that beer has played in world history and I might never have guessed that Christians would have loved beer as they did through the centuries or that they would have mastered the brewer's art with such conviction.

I was armed, then, as I approached the life of Arthur Guinness, with some important truths. I understood for the first time that beer had a noble history and that it had been intricately interwoven with the Christian faith for nearly seventeen hundred years by the time Arthur was born. I understood also that brewing had long been a respected profession and this was due in part to the positive contribution it made to society. Men drank beer rather than harder liquors, improved their health as they did—the B vitamins of beer being particularly important in times of meager diets—and in the post-Reformation centuries did so with a specific sense of offering their joys to God, as Calvin and Luther had taught them to do.

Thus I understood something I could not have before: that a convergence of brewing's evolution through history, the contributions of a Reformation view of the world, and the culture of the mid-1700s—in which a man could make his fortune but was encouraged to use it for the good of mankind—all of this built the perfect stage for the enterprising young man named Arthur Guinness and his particularly tasty brand of stout porter. For me, then, there was only one thing to do: I closed my books, packed my bags, and made off for the city of Dublin, the city from which young Arthur chose to make his mark upon the world.

Photo by Isaac Darnall

Dublin street scene today

THE RISE OF ARTHUR

I have often thought of that day years ago when I was wandering the glories of St. Paul's Cathedral in London and I came across the tomb of Christopher Wren. It was Wren, of course, who designed that magnificent building, along with fifty-five other London churches, after the Great Fire of 1666 forced the city to almost completely rebuild. Moved as I was by Wren's obvious genius, I was even more deeply touched by the words of his son, which were etched in a plaque on the wall of the great man's

The First Arthur Guinness

crypt. The inscription read, *Lector, si monumentum requiris circumspice.* The words meant, "Reader, if you seek his monument, look around you."

Those words have never left me. I have often thought of them as the ideal epitaph over a life well lived. What better tribute to a man, what better measure of a life, than that the good he has done is evident to all and so much so that it is visible from the very spot where he is buried.

My experience at the tomb of Christopher Wren came to mind when I visited Dublin years later to better understand the legacy of Arthur Guinness. You simply cannot escape the man, the company, and the good done by both in that teeming city on the River Liffey. Naturally, the famous Guinness sign, accompanied by the iconic signature of Arthur, is everywhere. Seemingly ever present, too, is the well-known painting of Arthur, his high forehead, aquiline nose, and powdered wig now embedded in the mind of most every Dubliner.

Yet it is more than advertising that makes Dublin for Arthur Guinness what St. Paul's in London is for Christopher

Wren. It is also the legacy of good that stands silent testimony on nearly every street and neighborhood square.

A visitor has only to walk past St. Patrick's Cathedral to learn that this noble church—built on the site where the great apostle first baptized new Christians in Ireland—was in horrible disrepair until Guinness money made its restoration possible. A bit further down the road is a lovely city park, St. Stephen's Green—again, a gift of Guinness. There are also the Roman Catholic churches that display plaques in honor of Arthur Guinness, a Protestant, for his outspoken defense of Roman Catholic rights. And then there is the group of homes that Guinness built, known to be of such quality that they will be standing—so I was told by a builder—a hundred years from now. Located in

The Liberties Rowhouses originally built for Guinness workers

the inner city neighborhood called "the Liberties," they are so wisely constructed that though they were first used to house Guinness workers, they are now cherished purchases by the Dublin stylish set.

The descriptions of Guinness benevolence—the buildings, institutions, trusts, parks, schools, and services that Guinness has left in its wake—could fill volumes. And we will learn more of these further on. Yet just as important as these monuments of stone and finance are the monuments that live in men's hearts. A hardened Dublin taxi driver tears up at the mention of the Guinness company. His grandmother, he tells me, might have died in her youth had Guinness doctors not tended her so well. And there is the aging scholar at Trinity College Dublin. He says he offers grateful prayers almost every day that his family went from laborers to educated middle class because brewery managers insisted that his gifted father reach beyond technical training alone and because Guinness money paid the cost. And now this man, this eminent and beloved scholar, tells everyone he can about the heritage of generosity that changed his family's life.

There is also the scruffy man outside the Guinness plant who stands beside his horse-drawn cart. He is covered in sawdust and feed and he knows he is an odd sight. He hopes you will want a picture of him, perhaps as a memento of Guinness days gone by. But when you take time to talk to him, you find he is not just a prop. He once worked for Guinness in his youth and he remembers the days well. Given how he looks, you expect complaints, maybe a list

of grievances unaddressed. Instead, he tells you how amazing it all was, and how the Guinness years were the best of his life. In fact, he is sad that his years at Guinness are done and he is a bit angry at the tide of change that has carried away the brewery he once knew. He tells you that he is not the only one who feels this way. Still, he insists that Guinness has always been the best place in Ireland to work. He hopes you will come back.

This is what you find, in the Dublin that is Arthur Guinness's monument, in the city that he loved and made his own. It is where the Guinness family chose to leave a legacy of benevolence, and why you find in stone and gratitude the record of a people who served their fellow man as they prospered, who built a cathedral of industry and philanthropy in honor of their God.

I have a favorite scene from the life of Arthur Guinness. It is likely not the one he would have chosen and it is not like any other that the slim record of his life reveals. Perhaps I like it because I am an American and I am naturally endeared to big personalities and crashing, passionate men. Perhaps, too, I find myself a bit hemmed in by the sketchy details of Arthur's life as I try to write his story. I've probably grown tired of how most of what we know of him comes to us from legal proceedings and government records. I want, as most of my generation do, a full-bodied treatment, a picture of a man who is liberated from the droning documents and the staid painting that I often feel imprison him. I want a man who comes before us red-blooded and bold.

This is why I've chosen this particular scene from his life as my favorite. It comes to us from 1771. Arthur is living in Dublin and has already purchased the run-down brewery with which he will make his name. And there is a conflict. It seems that on his own authority, Mr. Guinness has taken it upon himself to breach the walls of the watercourse and to increase the size of the pipes that carry water from the River Liffey to Arthur's land. But this is free, fresh city water and he is taking more than the authorities think he should. So when the Dublin Corporation's officers demand that he stop what amounts to a theft, Arthur fires back a message that says the water is his and he "would defend it by force of arms."

We like this man already.

Tensions mount and finally the city sheriff arrives. He brings with him a work crew whose orders are to fill in the breaches in the watercourse that this man Guinness has illegally made. Arthur is not there at the time but his men stand strong and resist until the sheriff threatens them with prison. Just when they start to relent, the owner arrives in a rage. The accounts we have from the time tell us that Arthur quickly sized up the situation, grabbed a pickaxe from one of his men, and "with very much improper language [declared] that they should not proceed . . . that if they filled [the watercourse] up from end to end, he would immediately re-open it."

Frankly, the story gets mundane from there. There is a lawsuit, it takes years to resolve, and by that time Arthur Guinness is one of the lead brewers of Dublin and too respectable for the sheriff to bully. Finally, a deal is made and Guinness receives all the water he needs for the slight sum of £10 a year.

Still, I like that dramatic moment with the pickaxe and all the more so because it feels to me that most of the rest of Arthur Guinness's life is concealed behind deeds and lawsuits, behind false legends and Irish myths. Concealing him, too, is that painting, the one that makes him seem to my American sensibilities like one of the duller founding fathers, like the kind of man Thomas Jefferson would have tipped his hat to on the street but never have invited to dinner. Arthur Guinness was a great deal more, though, and it is important that we try to glimpse of him what we can so that we may better understand who he was in his day and also how he laid a foundation for the family that graced the centuries after.

*   *   *

Had you listened to the gossips on the Dublin docks sometime in the early 1800s, you would have heard the tales of Arthur Guinness's father, of how he was the illegitimate son of an English soldier named Gennys and a willing Irish girl. Then, you might also have heard how this son, named Richard, grew up and became the groom of a family named Read. According to the rumors, it seems that one night Richard made off with the Reads' daughter, the lovely Elizabeth, never to return. And thus, "from the mists of time," as one historian wrote, came the Guinness family.

As romantic as all this is, it is very likely untrue. There is no evidence of an English soldier and an Irish girl, nor of Elizabeth Read eloping with the family groom.

What Arthur Guinness himself came to believe in later years was that his father was descended from Bryan Viscount Magennis of Iveagh, known to be from County Down. This Magennis was apparently a Catholic nobleman who supported James II at the unfortunate battle of the Boyne. Fleeing from Ireland to France in the aftermath of that encounter, Magennis left behind a branch of his clan who probably tried to protect themselves by dropping the prefix "Ma"—which means "the family"—and by converting to Protestantism. Thus, Arthur sprang from a Protestant clan named Gennis who later picked up an extra *s* in their name.

Although this is what Arthur believed, it is not a story we can confirm these centuries later. In fact, DNA analysis done at Trinity University in 2007 has suggested that the Guinnesses are descended from a family named McCartan who lived in a village called "Ginnies" in County Down. Historians continue to argue the matters. What we do know with some certainty from the few dusty documents we have is that Richard Guinness, father of Arthur, did marry an Elizabeth Read and then worked for the Reverend Dr. Arthur Price, the affluent Protestant vicar of Celbridge in County Kildare. We also know that in time, Dr. Price became Archbishop of Cashel and that as he rose in the world he took his good man Richard Guinness with him.

There are some matters we have to imagine, that we have to conjure from the few lines in a document here and the bit of oral tradition there. As the manager of Dr. Price's estate, Richard would have had many duties. He would have seen to the livestock, supervised the growing of crops, collected the rents from tenants, and assured that the buildings were in good repair. He would also have been responsible for the brewing of beer. It is here, then, on an archbishop's estate and under the tutelage of his father, that the future founder of the famed Guinness brewery surely first learned his trade.

We should understand that brewing at this time in Ireland was very much a cottage industry—almost literally. Housewives did it, estate managers did it, brewhouse owners did it and, of course, breweries did it, mostly along the winding waterways of Dublin. Beer was simply a staple of life in those days. In fact, we know that Arthur's grandfather, William Read, brewed beer. We know that he applied for a license to sell ale in 1690, and that this gives us the sole written link between beer and any of Arthur's ancestors. Undoubtedly, once William brewed his beer, he would have sold it from an ale tent at a spot along the Dublin-Cork road near where he lived. A single poetic sentence from Patrick Guinness's masterful *Arthur's Round: The Life and Times of Brewing Legend Arthur Guinness* paints the scene for us well: "We can picture a regiment struggling into the foothills several hours march south of Dublin on the rough, rutted, dusty main road and seeing a welcome ale tent with jugs of beer waiting to hit their thirsty palates." It was a meager beginning but it anticipated much that was to come.

This beer brewing by Arthur's grandfather Read was very much in the Irish tradition. We've already seen that Dioscorides—that first-century Greek botanist and physician—reported that the Hiberni drank a brewed barley liquid called *cuirim*. Many of the Irish myths and early documents mention the drink, including *Críth Gablach*, a law tract of the 700s that affirms a prince's routine as "Sunday for drinking ale, for he is no rightful prince who does not promise ale for every Sunday."

So important were beer and its effects among the Irish that the pagan high kings of the land had to symbolically marry the goddess-queen Medb (Maeve), whose name meant "the drunken" or "she who makes drunk." By drinking beer to excess at Tara—an ancient seat of the high kings of Ireland—these kings attained their sovereignty. It is no wonder that St. Patrick took his brewmaster, Mescan, with him as he tried to bring such pagan practices to an end. Beer was simply interwoven into all of Irish life; this was no less the case by the time of Richard Guinness. Though the Irish called whiskey *uisce beatha*—"the water of life"—by the early 1700s they were glad for the traditions that gave them a healthy and tasty drink that was only lightly intoxicating.

We should understand, then, that when Arthur Guinness came into the world—probably in 1724 at Dr. Price's Oakley Park estate in Celbridge—that world was often astir about beer. With brewing taking place in nearly every home, estate, and public house, recipes would have been closely guarded, new discoveries rumored and tried. Noble families would have had reputations for finely brewed beer and invitations to their tables would have been eagerly sought.

It is exactly in this way that Reverend Price's man, Richard, made something of a name for himself. It seems that the archbishop's estate was known for the dark beer that was brewed there, and many a guest tried to question the reverend's trusted agent to find out how he produced such a fine-tasting drink. Naturally, Richard, proud of his celebrated dark stout, would never say.

In the absence of solid information, myth and legend grew. Some said that Richard Guinness once accidentally roasted his barley too long and that the caramelized result was stronger and better than any other brew. Others said that the family had stolen the recipe from some monks whose beer "could make hairs grow on a man's chest." But of course, we know the truth now. Dark beer had been brewed before Arthur was even born. It was already

Oakley Park, Celbridge, 1902.

a favorite in London before the Guinness name was ever attached to a commercially sold brew, and it was a particular favorite among the city's porters, who gave this dark beer its name.

Though we do not know exactly how Richard Guinness came to brew a superior dark beer, we do know that it was the pride of Dr. Price and the envy of the archbishop's guests. Moreover, we can certainly imagine that Richard would have taught young Arthur the skills of brewing and this would have inaugurated one of the central themes in the Guinness story: mastery of craft passed from father to son.

For generations after Richard first began teaching young Arthur the brewing trade, Guinness son would work at Guinness father's side to master the lore and labors that would make for one of the finest beers and the most successful companies in the world. And this would not just be so in the Guinness family. There were also the farmers or seamen or grooms or cask makers who helped make Guinness beer—perhaps for five or six generations in a row—and who looked on the company's success as their own. Whole families of men would often labor side by side and then discuss the craft of brewing at night around their dinner tables, stirring in younger brothers and grandchildren an eagerness to take their places in the family profession. Skills perfected through decades and unlearnable from a book were passed from man to man, acquired in each generation by example and patient training, tools in hand. It was a legacy of mastery, a generational gift of experience and art, much of it now lost in our machine-dominated age but all of it honored through the centuries of Guinness men.

A Guinness historian has written that "infant Arthur would have inhaled the bracing smell of malt before he could walk." It was true. The boy would have lived in a world of brewers: his grandfather Read, his mother—who would certainly have brewed beer for her family—and, of course, his father, Richard, who brewed to meet the needs of the Price estate. It is not hard for us to imagine how Arthur would have grown into muscled adolescence shoveling the barley or carrying the water so essential to brewing. He certainly would have tended the fires necessary for boiling wort and for roasting. And he would have carried pails of beer to the thirsty on the estate and perhaps to favored friends of Dr. Price. He would have learned early that brewing is an art, that for many a man beer is an elixir, and that people in his day were willing to pay well those who could keep them in abundant supply.

Yet Arthur's education went far beyond the practical matters of estate management and the techniques for brewing beer. We know—again from the meager documents that are available—that by his late teens Arthur served Dr. Price as a registrar, a secretary-copyist of sorts. This tells us that Arthur must have mastered the reading, math, and penmanship that were regarded as essential to a man of affairs in that day. We can see this from Arthur's famous signature, which is now used in Guinness advertising around the world. Bold, confident, carefully styled, and technically sophisticated, it comes from the lease for St. James's Gate. Arthur must have learned this manner of writing in his childhood and teens, when a man's handwriting takes form. He must have mastered penmanship and perhaps other vital fields of knowledge at the Charitable School that was half a mile from his home. Then again, Dr. Price would certainly have had a personal library that he very likely would have allowed Arthur to use. He had agreed to be Arthur's godfather, after all, and we can see evidence that Dr. Price felt kindly about the boy and helped him advance whenever he could. Arthur may very well have reveled in the glories of Dr. Price's well-stocked library and may even have benefited from some mentoring by the archbishop as well. By the time Arthur was twenty, he was a smart, capable young man in Dr. Price's employ. He helped manage the affairs of the estate, witnessed documents, copied and filed, and certainly was involved in every aspect of brewing beer.

Arthur would remain in Dr. Price's employ until the archbishop's death in 1752. In his first decade of manhood, from his eighteenth year until he was twenty-eight, Arthur improved himself through labor but he also knew difficulty and pain. From 1739 through 1741, Ireland endured a period of the most severe weather on record. The cold was hardly to be believed. "Birds froze in mid-flight, crops failed, food shortages occurred and diseases followed,"

Patrick Guinness has written. Young Arthur would have seen this hardship, would likely have helped Dr. Price tend the needy, and would have learned firsthand what widespread suffering means. Then, in August of 1742, Arthur's mother, Elizabeth, died. She was only forty-four and she left behind six children and a husband who needed her dearly both as lover and friend but also as practical worker in the home. Arthur, too, only eighteen, would have suffered horribly from her loss.

This decade in Arthur's life would also have been filled with projects and plans. Dr. Price was ever coming up with new designs for the estate, with new ideas for the crops or experimental ways to increase the livestock. During this time, he even decided to take the roof off the ancient hilltop cathedral at Cashel, his ecclesiastical seat, thus creating one of the great ruins in Ireland. He was never able to rebuild, though he did construct a smaller cathedral nearby. The ruin remains to this day and offers visitors a chance to snicker at the often quixotic Dr. Price.

Still, whatever his faults, it was the generosity of Archbishop Price that made much possible for the Guinness family. When he died in 1752, Dr. Price left £100 to his faithful agent, Richard. This was a grand sum, equal to nearly four years' salary. But then, in an astonishing show of affection and largess, Arthur's godfather left him the same amount—£100. For a twenty-eight-year-old secretary and assistant manager, it was a gift that transformed private hopes into possibilities.

Now events would speed up in Arthur Guinness's life. Slightly more than three months after the archbishop's death, Richard Guinness married again, this time to an Elizabeth Clare, widow of Benjamin Clare, a Guinness family friend. Elizabeth ran the White Hart Inn at Celbridge and this soon became Richard's responsibility too. Arthur followed, and from 1752 to 1755, he honed his brewing skills by making the beer sold at the inn. He was nearing thirty, though, and had yet to make his mark. While he served his father and stepmother well, he likely harbored dreams of striking out on his own.

He took the first dramatic step toward his ambitions when in 1755 he purchased a small brewery in Leixlip, a village on the road from Celbridge to Dublin. He would only run this brewery for a few years before leaving it with his brother, Richard, and moving to Dublin to make his fortune, but we should not rush too quickly past this period in his life. Given who he would become, we can look back on these years and realize they were the times of perfecting and honing that a great man always requires. During this season, Arthur was going beyond the basics of brewing to a mastery of its mysteries.

Brewing was still unscientific at this time. Thermometers were only beginning to be used and yeast was barely even imagined by most brewers. Instead, there was much sniffing, much tasting of the ingredients, much going with feel as much as with thought. There were well-documented processes, yes, but a great beer could not be made according to charts and instruments alone. The technology simply wasn't sophisticated enough. So a young brewer like Arthur would have needed time to sharpen his senses, to watch older masters and to investigate brewing by trial and error. He needed the experience of brewing at the White Hart Inn and then at his small brewery in Leixlip. Still, he knew he was destined for more and so in 1759 he made his move to Dublin, a move that determined everything that came after in his life.

It is obvious, given the step he was about to take, Arthur had chosen brewing as his life's work. He may have felt something of a moral mandate for this. He was stepping onto a broader stage of brewing just as the Gin Craze was decimating much of his world. In 1689, Parliament had forbidden the importation of liquor. Unwilling to do without, the people of Ireland and England had begun making their own. By the early 1700s, one in every sixth house in London was a gin shop, some with signs proclaiming, *Drunk for one penny, dead drunk for two pence, clean straw for nothing.* For the lower classes, gin solved everything. It was fed to infants when they cried, given to children to make them sleep, and consumed to the point of intoxication by most every adult. It poisoned men's souls, making them lazy, mean, and wild. One bishop complained, "Gin has made the English people what they never were before—cruel and inhuman." So it was with the Irish, as well.

Two prints by William Hogarth tell the tale. In his

famous depictions of *Gin Lane* and *Beer Street*, it is the world dominated by gin that has fallen into disgrace. In *Gin Lane*, murder, suicide, hunger, and depravity prevail. Only the pawnbroker's house is in good repair. The distillery is owned by a Mr. Kilman, Hogarth's sly reference to what gin was doing to the people of his time. In *Beer Street*, though, all is orderly and clean and only the pawnbroker's house is in disrepair. Men drink beer while fishwives learn ballads, a basket of books near at hand. Clearly, this was the understanding at the time: gin destroys lives while beer is healthy and safe, enhancing rather than eroding good society. Arthur Guinness would have absorbed this lesson—from Hogarth, from Archbishop Price, and from his own moral evaluation of the world around him—and would have come to see his chosen profession as a service to his fellow man.

In 1759, Arthur made his move to Dublin. We should locate this moment clearly in time. It is the year that George Washington marries Martha Custis. The British Museum opens, the first life insurance company is begun in America, and British general James Wolfe begins the siege of Quebec and then loses his life on the Plains of Abraham. Composer George Frideric Handel dies this year but William Wilberforce the abolitionist is born, as is Scottish poet Robert Burns. Thomas Jefferson is a precocious sixteen-year-old, Voltaire's *Candide* is all the rage in Paris, and throughout Europe newspapers report that tea cups now usually have handles, a departure from the handleless oriental design.

It is a common error for writers of the Guinness story to draw a direct line between Dr. Price's gift of £100 and the purchase of the Guinness brewery at St. James's Gate in Dublin, as though the one made the other possible. This is far from the case, as we have seen. By the time Arthur moved to Dublin he was thirty-four. He had worked as Dr. Price's secretary and assistant for eight years. He had brewed beer in his stepmother's inn for three years. Then he had run a brewery of his own in Leixlip for nearly five years. The important matter is not that he used the £100 pounds to buy his brewery, because he did not, but rather that he made that gift even more valuable by investing it and adding to it his own skill and mastery of his trade. By 1759, then, he was able to do something exceptional, something that other men, perhaps even with the same resources, could not have managed to do.

In medieval Dublin there was an old gate to the city through which people passed on their way to the south and west of Ireland, some on pilgrimages to the holy sites of Europe. Called St. James's Gate because of the church and parish by that name nearby, it stood for nearly five centuries before crumbling to the ground. The name was retained for the location, though, largely because there had been a holy well on the site that was the centerpiece for an annual summer festival.

In 1610, Barnaby Rich described the site in his *New Description of Ireland* and one passage from this work is almost eerie given what St. James's Gate would one day be.

"On the west part of Dublin they have St. James, his Well," Rich wrote, "And his feast is celebrated the 25th of July, and upon that day, a great mart or fair is kept fast by the Well. The commodity that is there to be vended, is nothing else but ale, no other merchandise but only ale."

In 1759, there was a lapsed brewery on the site. (In fact, there had been a brewery there since 1670.) By the time Arthur Guinness walked the grounds to decide if he should buy it, the four-acre site included a brewhouse, a gristmill, two malt houses, and stables to accommodate a dozen horses. There was something else, too, something invisible that another man might have missed. There was the potential bound up in a city plan. For two years prior, work had

The Guinness brewery, as seen from
across the River Liffey today

been underway on Ireland's Grand Canal. The intention was to link Dublin with the River Shannon and thus with Limerick. If this plan was a success, it would put the terminus of the canal at James's Street in Dublin—nearly at Arthur Guinness's front door, should he decide on the purchase. A canal would provide the transport that a thriving brewery required and Arthur—ambitious and now skilled in evaluating investments—knew what the project might mean for whoever brewed beer at St. James's Gate. He decided it should be him.

On December 31, 1759, Arthur Guinness leased the property from the Rainsford family who owned it. The terms were £100 down and £45 a year, which was nothing exceptional. However, somehow Arthur talked the Rainsfords into giving him a lease for up to nine thousand years! It was one of the most unusual rental arrangements in history and it stands today as a symbol of Arthur's exceptional business acumen. It could be that the bold, swirling signature Arthur used to seal the lease—the signature now used in Guinness advertising—was a form of celebration. He would certainly have been entitled.

Thrilled with the deal he had made, Arthur went to work. He hired men, bought horses, ordered work crews to fix up the grounds and the buildings, and got his brewery brewing. It was, as most new ventures are, slow going at first. We can jump ahead in the story and mention that in 1779 Guinness became the official provider of beer to Dublin Castle, the headquarters of the British government in Ireland. This is a revealing statement of how much Arthur Guinness had risen in the world and how fine his beer had become. But this was twenty years later, after struggles and lean years and haunting doubts about whether the venture would survive. That it did and did gloriously should not blind us to the character required to make it all work, the long hours, and the fortitude of soul that a risky, expensive business launch demands.

While he fashioned his new brewery to fit his dream, he also made a move that lifted him to new heights in Dublin society. On June 17, 1761, Arthur married Olivia Whitmore. For the young brewer, it was a brilliant decision, love and romance aside. First, she was half his age and known to be a radiant beauty. Second, she was wealthy. Her parents were gentry and her dowry was just over £1000, a huge sum for

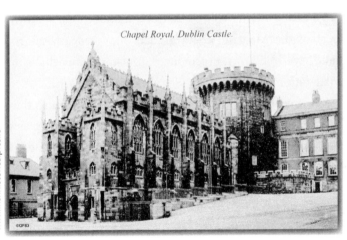

Dublin Castle

the day. Perhaps as important, she would bring to Arthur's life connections and status in Dublin society that he might never have acquired on his own. Olivia was related to the leading families of the city: the Darleys and the LeTouches of banking fame and the Smyths, whose lineage included an archbishop and more than one lord mayor. It was the perfect match for a rising young businessman, measured purely by practical standards.

Arthur also brought significant weight to the marriage. He was obviously a man looked upon as having great potential or Olivia's family would never have approved. Also, he had recently claimed the Magennis clan as his own, though historians often grumble that this was a self-aggrandizing choice without any historical merit. Still, the connection was so dear to Arthur and so valued by his new in-laws that they presented him at his wedding with a silver cup bearing the newlywed couple's names along with the crest of the Magennises—a golden boar beneath the red hand, symbolic of the province of Ulster from which the Magennises arose.

Two years after the wedding, Olivia gave birth to their first child, Elizabeth, and two years later, Hosea, their first son, was born. All together there would be ten children, four girls and six boys: Elizabeth, Hosea, Arthur, Edward, Olivia, Benjamin, Louisa, John Grattan, William Lunell, and Mary Anne. What this happy list of deeply loved children does not betray is there were actually twenty-one pregnancies but Olivia miscarried eleven times. She must have been a sturdy, courageous woman. Despite her losses, she kept having children until 1781, when she was in her late forties. Her last child was born when her oldest was already married.

And so the dynasty began. Arthur now rose in Dublin society, joined clubs and organizations, and became a voice for brewing in political life. In time, he bought a Georgian mansion, called Beaumont House, in which he lived nearly until the day he died. He also became the warden of the Dublin Corporation of Brewers. He was, by every measure, a success. Before he died in 1803, he would see his ramshackle little brewery grow into the biggest business enterprise in Ireland.

Yet what distinguishes the Arthur Guinness story is not just that he brewed good beer and sold great amounts of it. What distinguishes his story is that he understood his success as forming a kind of mandate, a kind of calling to a purpose of God beyond just himself and his family to the broader good he could do in the world. To understand this, though, we must understand the religious influences that shaped Arthur Guinness's life.

For thousands of years before St. Patrick introduced Christianity into Ireland, the Gaels—an ancient Celtic people—had lived their bold and pagan ways in that land.

From the fifth century, these Gaels ruled the island politi-
cally until the twelfth century, the few episodes of Viking
invasion aside. In 1172, King Henry II of England invaded
Ireland and the English thus claimed all of Ireland for
the next seven hundred years. In actuality, though, the
English only ruled a few coastal cites and the Pale, the
area immediately surrounding Dublin. In the sixteenth
century, English control expanded until finally the old
Gaelic social and political structures collapsed. This was
also the time of the Protestant Ascendancy, the rise of
a new English ruling class, following the separation of
the English church from Rome by Henry VIII in 1534.
What resulted was an Ireland ruled by a small minority
of English Protestants. Catholics, though they constituted
90 percent of the population, owned less than 10 percent
of the land and were barred from the Irish Parliament.
We should remember here that had Arthur Guinness been
Roman Catholic, he would never have been allowed to
buy his brewery.

The tensions and resentments that this situation produced were seldom quelled. An illustration comes to us from
the journals of the evangelist George Whitefield, who tried
to speak in Dublin two years before Arthur started his life
there. Whitefield had received permission to speak on a green
near the Dublin barracks and as he did he felt his message
"go forth in power." There was the usual opposition—a few
stones or dirt clods thrown for effect while he spoke—but
this was nothing new. Whitefield had learned to preach while

people banged drums or drove cattle through his crowds. Once he spoke while a man urinated on him from a tree. He knew what it was to have his message opposed.

In Dublin, though, the raging torrent against him was worse than any he had known. As he made his way from his pulpit, "vollies of hard stones came from all quarters, and every step I took a fresh stone struck, and made me reel backwards and forwards." These missiles came from "hundreds and hundreds of papists," he recalled. Soon he was "almost breathless, and all over a gore of blood . . . I received many blows and wounds; one was particularly large and near my temples . . . for a while I continued speechless, panting for and expecting every breath to be my last." Finally, Whitefield was rescued by a Methodist preacher and tended by a local surgeon. We should remember that at the time Whitefield was a clergyman in the Church of England and one of the most famous men in the world, and yet he was nearly killed by an anti-Protestant crowd within easy view of British troops.

By the time Arthur Guinness moved to Dublin, he was a loyal Protestant son of the Church of Ireland who had been well educated in religious matters on the estate of an influential archbishop. As he rose in Dublin society, he evidenced a deeply Christian and nonconformist conscience. He spoke out against anti-Catholic laws and he thought nothing of challenging the traditions of the ruling class when morality was involved. He once argued against the traditional feasting of a new alderman because such occasions most always resulted in drunkenness and carousing. He thought the city fathers should set a moral example.

Adding to the values he had absorbed from his upbringing, Arthur was also influenced by the great religious innovator, John Wesley. We know that Wesley preached at Arthur's church while Arthur was in attendance. Wesley seemed to have been unimpressed with the experience. "Oh who has the courage to speak plain to these rich and honorable sinners!" Wesley intoned after speaking to the congregation at St. Patrick's Cathedral. Apparently, Wesley found the fashionable church filled with wealthy, calloused souls.

Still, some members of the church were deeply stirred by Wesley's message and his Methodist movement. Among them was William Smyth, who came from a wealthy Dublin family and whose uncle was the archbishop of Dublin. He was also Arthur's relative, since Olivia Guinness was William's wife's cousin. Smyth helped to build Bethesda Chapel—"the great center of Irish evangelicalism"—and traveled with Wesley often, even introducing him to the rich and powerful of Dublin. Certainly, Arthur Guinness would have been among them and it is not assuming too much to believe that Arthur not only met Wesley on several occasions but often heard him speak. Indeed, Wesley's journal repeatedly mentions meetings at which Arthur was almost certainly present.

Oddly, though, the great preacher was again less than thrilled with what he saw. One mention of a meeting under Smyth's direction is typical. "Mr. Smyth read prayers, and gave out the hymns," Wesley wrote, "which were sung by fifteen or twenty fine singers; the rest of the congregation listening with much attention and as much devotion as they would have done to an opera. But is this Christian worship? Or ought it ever to be suffered in a Christian church?"

Despite Wesley's disappointments with the fledgling evangelical church in Ireland, there is little doubt that he had a profound influence on Arthur. This came not just from Wesley's insistence upon a transforming brand of salvation, but also from evangelical social teaching that meshed with what was already in Arthur's heart. We must recall that Methodism was conceived in evangelical social outreach. The tiny Holy Club at Oxford, which became the first society (or small group) of Methodism, included John and Charles Wesley and George Whitefield, to name but a few. This group perfected holiness by visiting prisoners, taking up collections for the poor, and urging the rich to fulfill their Christian obligations to society. Whitefield alone founded orphanages, funded feeding centers, and even challenged the traditional relations between slave owners and slaves when he visited America. Wesley did much the same and worked to make each of his societies an agent of social good. He also preached both the virtues and the responsibilities of wealth. "We must exhort all Christians to gain all they can and to save all they can; that is, in effect to grow rich," Wesley insisted. Yet the corollary was that this gaining of wealth was to allow the Christian man to "give all he can to those in need."

Though we cannot know the precise degree of connection between John Wesley and Arthur Guinness, we do know that Arthur lived out Wesley's social values for the rest of his life. He was, as we've seen, a champion of rights for Roman Catholics in Ireland and he modeled this conviction by his treatment of his own Catholic workers. This was at a time when such views might easily have cost him customers and standing in society. He was, too, on the board of Meath Hospital for many years and he eventually became its governor, in charge of assuring that the "relief of the poor in the Earl of Meath's Liberties" was fully supported. He also joined an organization called the Friendly Brothers of St. Patrick, whose aim was the abolition of dueling, still a source of widespread scandal at the time. Beyond these associations, he supported a variety of charities and even promoted Gaelic arts and culture as a means of instilling an ennobling sense of heritage in his countrymen.

Some historians have concluded that these efforts were merely the attempts of a middle-class merchant to impress his betters with good works. There may be some truth in this. Arthur was indeed ambitious and would not have wanted to seem lacking in the generosity expected of a rising merchant in Georgian Dublin. Still, there was another favorite project of his that seems confirmation of both the purity of his faith and his concern for social good: he was the founder of the first Sunday schools in Ireland.

Arthur was influenced in this by the famous educational reformer Robert Raikes. Born in Gloucester, the city of George Whitefield's birth, in 1736, Raikes was the son of a newspaperman who published the *Gloucester Journal*. After inheriting the publishing business from his father in 1757, Raikes grew alarmed at the state of children in the slums of England and began using his paper to draw attention to the plague of grinding poverty and vicious crime that tormented England's cities.

Having some knowledge of the prison system, he concluded that vice was "better prevented than cured." He therefore became convinced that education was the key and created a system for offering instruction on Sundays in Bible, reading, and other basic subjects to the children of the poor. As a devoted Anglican, Raikes believed that basic education, combined with the leavening work of Scripture and church attendance, would change lives for the better. The movement spread rapidly, though it was opposed by conservatives who viewed Raikes as a meddler and by Sabbatarians who thought it a sin to conduct a school on Sundays.

As Raikes described the curriculum, "The children were to come after ten in the morning, and stay till twelve; they were then to go home and return at one; and after reading a lesson, they were to be conducted to Church. After Church, they were to be employed in repeating the catechism till after five, and then dismissed, with an injunction to go home without making a noise." Though critics dubbed the effort "Raikes's Ragged School," by 1831 Sunday schools in Great Britain were ministering to more than 1.25 million children, which was approximately one-quarter of the population of poor children in England at the time. Others emulated Raikes's methods, notably Hannah Moore in Somerset; of course, Raikes is celebrated today as the father of the Sunday school movement worldwide.

Arthur Guinness became a champion of the Sunday school cause. In 1786, he extended Raikes's work to Ireland by organizing the first Sunday school in Dublin. The slim records we have show that Arthur funded the effort nearly by himself in the early days, did much of the organizing work alone at first, and spoke often to gatherings of his merchant friends to solicit their help. Given that he risked offending Roman Catholics, grumbling conservatives, the comfortable, and even Sabbatarians by his efforts, Arthur's courageous devotion to this movement says much about what he was willing to brave to fulfill his sense of calling in the world.

Yet none of these efforts would have been possible or noteworthy had Arthur Guinness not been skilled at brewing beer. We should visualize him at this time in his life as busy with his various social causes, yes, but also in constant search of how best to improve his standing in the competitive world of brewing. There would be much tasting and sniffing and fingering of ingredients. Frequent conversations with his men and much culling of brewing talk at his clubs would have helped as well. He would draw, too, from the wisdom of his forebears: from the brewing legacy of Grandfather Read, his mother, and of course his father,

Richard, now dead since 1766. He would have learned to trust himself, as well, given that he now had decades of valuable experience to lean upon.

Still, he had yet to make the shift that would win him world renown. He was still brewing both ale and the dark stout that had become quite the fashion. In his history with the brew that he would be associated with for generations to come, he is confirmation that the race is not to the swift or the battle to the strong. He was not the first or the best or the only brewer to produce dark porter at this time. But he was, perhaps, the most consistent, the most willing to ride the currents of his age, and he was blessed with good timing. If history favors the bold over the most gifted, then Arthur is certainly encouragement to those who are willing to be the former in recognition that they are incapable of being the latter.

Arthur was not the first to brew porter, as we have seen. That distinction likely goes to Ralph Harwood Shoreditch in London, who was already brewing a dark beer two years before Arthur was born. This early effort had the unappetizing name of "Entire Butt," a butt being a barrel and the word *entire* referring to the combination of three types of beer in one barrel to produce the desired effect. The beer was immediately popular. By 1727, when Arthur was but three, a Swiss visitor to England wrote, "The greater quantity of this beer is consumed by the working classes. It is a thick and strong beverage and the effect it produces, if drunk to excess, is that of wine. This 'porter' costs threepence a pot. In London there are a number of alehouses where nothing but this sort of beer is drunk."

The celebrated strength of this dark beer was easily explained. Brewers, in the unending experimentation that was part of brewing life in that day, had learned to use extra portions of charred malt and barley to give their beer both body and color. More hops than usual were employed, as well, to add flavor and to help preserve the brew over time. The art, though, was in gaining more from the ingredients by prolonging the mashing, boiling, and fermentation process. The result was a more robust and stable beer that could be stored longer and would survive the jostling of export without going bad.

Arthur did not quickly rest his reputation on this new dark porter as some other brewers did. English price controls gave English brewers a distinct advantage over Irish brewers, particularly in production of porter, and so in his early days at St. James's Gate, Arthur brewed almost exclusively Irish ale. At some point, probably before 1783, he began brewing the dark beer that was becoming so popular. We can see in the *Journals of the Irish House of Commons* that by this same year, 1783, Arthur took pride in his association with dark beer, for as he said in testimony before a parliamentary committee, "a porter brewer buys nothing but the best, as nothing else will answer." By 1799, though, he had made up his mind. He brewed his last ale on April 22, and from then on St. James's Gate became a "porter brewery."

Now the race was as much with the legally favored English brewers as it was with brewers at home. Fortunately, competition motivates, usually improving both product and service in the fight for market share. This seems to have been the case at St. James's Gate, for as Jonathan Guinness wrote in his moving *Requiem for a Family Business*,

In Arthur's day brewing was still an art, not a science . . . there were no laboratories to analyze samples of barley and hops; the brewer's eye was the only measuring tool. As to yeast, it is a living organism, and a quick-breeding one; and even now with strict scientific control it can develop a genetic mutation so inconvenient as to require the destruction of an entire batch. Arthur must have mastered all these problems better than most. In particular, he was among the first Irishmen to become really good at producing the black porter. Once Arthur Guinness and the other Irish brewers—he had competitors—had cracked the technical problem and produced a porter as good as that which came from London, it was worth their while to concentrate on it. Soon the Irish product not only equaled the London porter, but surpassed it; after conquering the Dublin market, Irish porter became in demand in Britain.

We should not ignore here one of the great factors in the rise of great men: timing. Just as the St. James's Gate brewery was hitting its stride, Ireland began enjoying a period of independence from England that was a result both of the American Revolution and the efforts of famed Irish statesman—and Olivia Guinness's cousin—Henry Grattan. A new Constitution in 1782 gave Ireland freedom from political and economic restrictions that had been imposed since medieval times. Ireland would now enjoy seventeen years of unprecedented legislative freedom, an era that is known to later history as the age of Grattan's Parliament.

Arthur certainly benefited from this era of freedom, as did all in the rising merchant class, but he was also well served by Henry Grattan's support for Irish brewing. In a letter to Arthur, Grattan wrote that the Irish brewing industry was "the natural nurse of the people and entitled to every encouragement, favor and exemption." Political winds could not have been blowing in a better direction for Arthur and at just the time when several other forces were converging in his favor: the political benefits of his marriage, his retooling of the brewery, his mastery of the brewing trade, and his reputation as an exceptional man.

There would be political storms ahead, of course. Rather than continue on the path of allowing Ireland further freedom, England would eventually reverse herself and force an Act of Union in 1801. This act would abolish self-government and merge Ireland into the United Kingdom led by the same foolish monarch who had already lost the American colonies. Ireland would fight for her liberty for more than another hundred years—sad, tragic years of blood and bitterness.

Yet through these years, Arthur Guinness and his growing family prospered. The brewery at St. James's Gate thrived. Arthur added on, innovated, hired the best men, and dreamed of greater brewing glory. He was already an admired man, having risen high in Dublin society and in respect among his fellow brewers. He continued to serve his beloved social causes and saw each of them do far-reaching good. Sunday schools dotted the land; Meath Hospital grew and served the poor well; the frequency of duels declined; and many of the causes Arthur supported met with stunning success.

Even in old age, he was beset with a classic brewer's disease: the need to experiment and reach for that better brew. Having made the decision to brew only porter, he then began brewing a number of variations on the dark beer theme. There was "Town Porter," intended for sale in and near Dublin. There was also "Country Porter" for the far regions of Ireland. Then, too, there was "Keeping Porter," which was brewed for blending with other beers and, finally, "Superior Porter," which was a strong beer available in all markets.

As late as December 1801, little more than a year before he died, he wrote in his brewer's notebook of an idea for "West India Porter." It would be higher in hops and alcohol than his other brews, he envisioned—thus allowing it to survive long journeys overseas—and it would be intended for export to the Caribbean as the name for the beer suggests. It was a brilliant idea, one fit for the times, and we even know how he began to brew it from the notes that he kept. His West India Porter would combine seventy-five parts black malt to fifty-five parts pale malt with twenty parts brown malt. It was an innovation, and Guinness scholars conclude that this unique recipe makes West India Porter the direct precursor to the Foreign Extra Stout that is still brewed today. It was the beginning, then, of the oldest continuously brewed beer in the world.

Arthur Guinness passed from this life on January 23, 1803. His children would go on to lead the brewery he founded to new heights; the cause of caring for the less fortunate to the greater glory of God would also live on in the Guinness generations to come. Arthur would certainly have been pleased, though the eventual global reach of the ramshackle brewery he leased in 1759 could certainly have never entered his mind.

Yet, as the master brewer he was, he would have been especially pleased with one of his contributions that lives on to this day. It is not the kind of legacy most other men would have understood, but Arthur Guinness and men of his kind—men who had felt their newly harvested barley and who knew the smell of malt and who could tell a good wort by the taste—would have nodded in knowing respect.

You see, the yeast that is used to brew beer is unique. It is not like the yeast used for bread, which dies at high temperatures, never to be used again. Instead, the yeast used for brewing beer grows in the process and can be skimmed off and used again and again. This was such a miraculous discovery to early brewers that they gave this reusable yeast the nickname "God-is-good."

It is a moving tale and one of the legendary characteristics of brewing beer, but there is a more important point to the story. When Arthur went to Dublin to set up shop at St. James's Gate, he carried with him a Kildare strain of yeast that he had likely first used at the White Hart Inn. That strain, in turn, may have been one developed or used by his father, Richard, on Dr. Price's estate. So when Arthur went to Leixlip and then on to Dublin, he carried the descendant cells of yeast with him. In time, this strain would make its way to Guinness breweries around the world and thus down through the generations would go to work in Malaysia and Nigeria and Trinidad and even the United States. And today, 250 years later—despite the fact the Guinness is brewed in great computerized factories of stainless steel and by PhD technicians wearing lab coats—the original strain of Arthur's yeast is still at work "festering away in the oldest tuns, dating from even before 1760."

And so his labors live, not just in the brewery and in the faith and generosity of the Guinnesses who followed him, but also in the very beer that was his life's work. It is pleasant to think about how he might have enjoyed the thought that his yeast—grown in wooden vats and gently tended when many of the nations where it is sold today did not yet exist—has helped produce the nearly ten million pints a day of Guinness stout consumed in the modern world.

Author at the historic St. James's Gate Brewery

AT THE SAME PLACE
BY THEIR ANCESTORS

There is a theme in the affairs of men that has always been a source of wonderment to me. I found myself thinking about it often as I sat in the Guinness Archives at St. James's Gate, researching the descendants of Arthur who filled the nineteenth century.

What troubles me is this: a man becomes famous because of his character and skill. Or perhaps, as Shakespeare wrote, he simply has fame thrust upon him. His deeds are celebrated, his words remembered and rehearsed. He is revered. Then, at the end of his life, as his flame begins to fade, all eyes turn to his children. And the question becomes, Will the children prove themselves as gifted? Will they fulfill the mandate of their parent's fame?

As often as not, the children of the great fall short of their potential, fail to live up to the hopes that have surrounded them nearly from birth. Though some honor their parents' reputation by how they live, many come to regard their name as a burden—even a curse. It is painful to watch and perhaps in part because there seems to be no pattern. Loving parents are as likely to have children who despise their legacy as are parents of the more distant and neglectful kind.

The stories of these generational tensions could fill volumes, but a few examples make the point. There is the family line of the venerated American founding father, John Adams. Though his descendants include the brilliant statesman John Quincy Adams, the unfolding of the generations that followed this great man is a story of such decline that the leading book on the subject is titled *Descent from Glory*.

Then there was Winston Churchill, whose father, slipping daily into madness, hated his son and cursed him as a "public school wastrel." Winston was haunted throughout his life by the specter of this disapproving figure and determined to make a better life with his own son, Randolph. The early years were sweet and full of hope and expectation. But the relationship soured and Randolph, given to drunkenness and rage, was even banned from his parents' home during the dark years of World War II, when a father might have needed a loyal son. Finally, Randolph's life came to an end, as one historian has said, "beneath hope, beneath promise, and nearly beneath notice."

Oddly, even when the sons might bring honor and pride, the fathers are often unable to see it. Abraham Lincoln's oldest son, Robert, was clearly not his father's favorite, his deepest affection being reserved for the younger Willie and Tad. So Lincoln kept his distance and friends recounted that he once said "he guessed Bob would do no better than he had." Yet greatness was in Robert Lincoln, whether his father saw it or not. He would eventually graduate from Harvard, serve as his nation's Secretary of War and ambassador to the Court of St. James's, and ultimately chair the board of one of the most successful companies of his day. His was a life well lived, but his famous father never thought it might be so and did not live to see the promise fulfilled.

There are, of course, those cases where sons and daughters follow on in the way of the family name and bring honor to all that has come before, but these tend to be the exceptions that prove the truth that there is no certain pattern, no way of knowing whether what survives a man will win respect or shame. It seems that the best anyone can do, famous or not, is to love and embed values and then offer to God what cannot be controlled in a child's life. Perhaps this is the lesson: each generation stands on its own and there is only so much that those who come before them can do to assure a pleasing outcome.

I thought of this conclusion as I sat in the Guinness Archives and pondered the generations that unfolded after Arthur's death. He had done more than most to provide for his ten children, but he could not control their outcome, could not assure the character in each of them that is essential to success. So he did the most that any parent can do: he treated them generously and he committed them to God. Some would rise to his hopes. Some would struggle all their days in ways that would have broken his heart. And some, tragically, would live far beneath their material and spiritual legacy. In this, the Guinnesses were like most other families, though their fame and wealth would make their unfolding story one of the great generational tales of all time.

Arthur Guinness was buried on a cold January day in 1803. His funeral procession began at his beloved home, Beaumont House, on the north side of Dublin Bay, and rolled through the streets of that thriving city before turning inland. He had chosen to be buried next to his mother, at Oughterard in County Kildare. His gravestone read, "In the adjoining Vault are deposited the mortal remains of Arthur Guinness, late of James's Gate in the city and of Beaumont in the County of Dublin Esquire who departed his life on the 23rd of January AD 1803." It was a subdued epitaph for the man of whom the *Dublin Evening Post* wrote, "The worthy and the good will regret him because his life has been useful and benevolent and virtuous."

Fascinating are the lives of the children who gathered that day to mourn their father's death. There was, first, Hosea, the oldest son. It was his privilege to preside over his father's funeral because he was a clergyman, a respected minister in the Church of Ireland. Though as the first son he would naturally have inherited his father's role as head of the thriving brewery, Hosea had instead chosen the church. Arthur was surely glad that a deep faith lived in his oldest son, but he may have been less thrilled with the limited financial prospects of a minister's life. As he wryly wrote in his will, his oldest son would inherit the family home of Beaumont because he was "not in any line of life whereby he is likely by Industry to enlarge his Property."

Hosea was born in 1765, when his father was already a respected figure in Dublin society. Having chosen life in the church early on, Hosea attended Winchester College and Oxford before earning his BA and LLD at Trinity College in Dublin, but a few miles from St. James's Gate. He became the rector of the parish of St. Werburgh and lived in that city until his death in 1841.

From a distance it may seem as though Hosea lived a uniquely graced life. He was certainly an esteemed member of the Guinness clan who continued his father's social concerns by arguing for Catholic equality and sometimes championing the cause of the lower classes. He was also a scholar and classicist, who went so far as to name one of his sons Vicesimus. For many years, Hosea applied his academic skills to trying to establish the Guinness lineage, particularly their claim as part of the Magennis line. Some have seen this as an odd pursuit for a clergyman, but it shows his pride in his father's work and his devotion to his famous family's place in history.

Yet as blessed as Hosea's life seemed to be, there was also much suffering. His wife bore him twenty children, only six of whom survived to adulthood. One historian has written that the "melancholy procession of small coffins must have imparted a certain somberness to life at the rectory."

Then, too, there were the financial pressures. As a Church of Ireland minister, Hosea's salary was paid by tithes. Since 1801, when the Act of Union had disbanded the Irish Parliament and united the established church, tithes had been required of all citizens. This meant, of course, that Roman Catholics were forced to pay tithes to a church they despised. In protest, they often refused to pay at all, and this would leave clergymen like Hosea in dire financial straits. It was a story that was to replay itself again and again in Guinness history, for many Guinness descendants became clergymen. Because they had become accustomed to a certain standard of living and because their salaries were often woefully inadequate, they turned to their brewery relatives for help. This frequently became a heavy burden to those who tended the firm at St. James's Gate.

Even Guinnesses outside of the church and whose prospects seemed bright often found themselves turning, in time, to the company for aid. Elizabeth, the oldest child of Arthur and Olivia Guinness, was among these. She had married well. Her husband was the builder and quarry-master Frederick Darley. In 1809, Darley became the lord mayor of Dublin and this made Elizabeth the city's First Lady, a role that suited her perfectly. During these years, the Darleys prospered, primarily because the wars of that time created a demand for goods and services the Darleys could provide. In time, though, the wars ended and inflation ravaged Ireland. Frederick and Elizabeth ended up turning to the family company for help, which they received; again, it is a pattern that is repeated often in Guinness history.

Of Arthur Guinness's other daughters, the story is much the same. Olivia aside—who was born in 1775 but died when quite young—the two other daughters, Louisa and Mary Anne, each received £2,000 from their father upon his death; but both married clergymen who suffered the same financial troubles as Hosea and also turned to the company time and again.

Perhaps the most troubling story among those of Arthur's children is that of Edward Lee, who also stood there by the grave at Oughterard grieving his father's death. Handsome and charming, Edward was the kind of man who inspired confidence that his character could not sustain. Though the family hoped he would make his mark in the field of law, and eagerly sent him to the best schools for training, by his thirties Edward had not proven himself a capable man. Michele Guinness, in her insightful *The Genius of Guinness*, has written of Edward that he was "weak and indecisive, easily enticed by gracious living, without enough self-discipline to earn it . . . At thirty-one Edward had not yet distinguished himself in any way. Life was the problem. It failed him, or so he complained. Every family has a black sheep and Edward was the first of a long line."

It is not a flattering portrait, particularly when held up against a newspaper account of the day. One Dublin paper reported of him, "He gave bread to several hundred fellow creatures, who prospered under his auspices . . . he was candid and honorable in his dealings, highly esteemed and respected not only as a merchant but as a private gentleman." Such were the conflicting views of the man.

What we know with certainty, though, is that Edward decided to invest in a bold ironworks scheme that he thought a sure thing given the demands of war. Clearly, he had realized that he would never succeed at law and so he borrowed heavily and sank all his capital into a plan for ironworks at Palmerston and Lucan. Completely lacking any business skills, by 1811, he was bankrupt and the size of his debts staggered the mind. The family members who ran the brewery tried to help him but debts such as his were beyond their range. They simply could not clean up the mess and finally Edward was forced to flee to the Isle of Man, a kind of debtors' island at the time, where the law protected him from prosecution.

It was a huge blow to the family reputation. A son of

Arthur Guinness, brother of the rector of St. Werburgh, had betrayed his creditors and left mountainous debts. Tragically, Edward spent the rest of his days on the Isle of Man, firing off ever more desperate appeals for funds to his family in Ireland. This was not among the more noble episodes in Guinness history, but perhaps it is a valley that makes the heights of that history all the more meaningful.

With his sisters either passed away, married to unsuccessful businessmen, or bound to clergymen ever in need of assistance, and with most of his brothers either clergymen or foolish investors, the burden of both the family and the brewery fell upon Arthur Guinness II, who is often called Second Arthur. He, along with his younger brothers Benjamin and William Lunell, would not only preserve the brewery but prepare it for a much grander role on the world stage in the decades to come.

The second Arthur inherited the proprietorship of the family business at St. James's Gate when he was thirty-five years old. By that time, he had already spent a decade in apprenticeship to his father, as would be the Guinness habit. That decade was a most opportune time to learn the family trade, for during those years the Guinness firm became the largest of Dublin's brewing companies. In 1800, the brewery had sold some 10,026 thirty-six-gallon barrels of beer. Just three years later, by 1803, that number had doubled. In addition, the two Arthurs had presided over a vast plant expansion and had together made the strategic decision to stop brewing ale in order to concentrate on porter.

The confidence the first Arthur had in his son is evidenced by the change in name of the Guinness enterprise. Originally, the firm was known as "Arthur Guinness, brewer and flour dealer." This latter role came from Arthur's purchase and management of a flour mill in nearby Kilmainham. Obviously the Guinnesses had hopes that the flour business would one day match the success of the brewery. Shortly after this name appeared in the Dublin City Directory, though, the firm's name was changed in the listing to "Guinness, Arthur and Son, brewers." This revision occurred in 1794, the year that young Arthur joined his father in the trade.

Tremendous success graced the early years of the second Arthur's role as head of the brewery. Though at the time he took the lead, Guinness beer was primarily sold within a day's ride of Dublin, Arthur shared his father's dream of expanding the firm's markets and making Guinness a name brand around the world. Typically, he took counsel, planned, and then executed. By 1816, brewery records contained the boast that Guinness porter "successfully rivaled the London product even in the English metropolis." But Arthur still wasn't satisfied. He had helped develop the idea for West India Porter and now he wanted to make his new product a star in the Guinness line. Before long, Guinness was being shipped to Barbados, Trinidad, and even to Sierra Leone in West Africa.

Arthur's efforts to expand Guinness's markets paid off. Not only was the company realizing astonishing profits, but the Guinness name was becoming a noted brand throughout the English-speaking world. Casks of brew were shipped "wherever British troops were serving, and to wherever British expatriates were living." The brand became particularly popular among soldiers, grateful for a taste of home on far-off battlefields. In *Long Forgotten Days*, Ethel M. Richardson reported words from the journal of a British cavalry officer wounded at Waterloo:

> When I was sufficiently recovered to be permitted to take some nourishment, I felt the most extraordinary desire for a glass of Guinness, which I knew could be obtained without difficulty. Upon expressing my wish to the doctor, he told me I might take a small glass . . . It was not long before I sent for the Guinness and I shall never forget how much I enjoyed it. I thought I had never tasted anything so delightful. I am confident that it contributed more than anything else to the renewal of my spirit.

Over the next decades, the Guinness name appeared in Charles Dickens's *Pickwick Papers* and was endorsed by the editors of the *Morning Post*. "Guinness's Dublin Stout," the *Post* article stiffly proclaimed, "is confidently recommended for home consumption and for export, and must, from its age, purity and soundness, ensure the approbation and support of the Public." Even Prime Minister Benjamin Disraeli sang the praises of the brand. In a letter to his sister written on November 21, 1837, the celebrated statesman reported, "There was a division on the Address in Queen Victoria's first Parliament, 509 to 20. I then left the House at ten o'clock, none of us having dined . . . I supped at the Carlton, with a large party, off oysters and Guinness, and got to bed at half-past twelve o'clock. Thus, ended the most remarkable day hitherto of my life."

While the fame of Guinness grew, tumultuous economic times made the second Arthur's leadership of the firm difficult indeed. There was, first, the end of the Napoleonic War, which meant three hundred thousand men suddenly released from the army and constricting markets for munitions and military wares. As is often the case when a major military effort comes to an end, unemployment rose, business declined, and inflation soared. The United Kingdom entered a period of economic depression and Ireland, as usual, suffered most of all. Adding to Irish woes, the potato crop failed in 1817 and 1819, a harbinger of even greater suffering to come.

The brewing trade slumped, as well. Guinness had known its best year to date in 1815, when it produced a record 66,672 barrels of brew. Yet, just eight years later, in 1823, the company produced only 27,185 barrels, its worst year since 1804. Through patience and wise management, Guinness would return to its former heights, though it would not do so for many years.

The second Arthur thrived personally during these years, though he bore burdens that would have crushed lesser men. He had married Anne Lee in 1793, the daughter of Benjamin Lee of Merrion, and by all accounts the union was happy. The couple had three sons: William, born in 1795, Arthur Lee, born in 1797, and Benjamin Lee, born in 1798. It was also during this time that Arthur's business skills won him a respected role in the field of banking. In 1818, he was appointed the deputy governor of the Bank of Ireland and in 1820 he became its governor. It was a good fit for his temperament and he thrived. Though eventually this role would pull him away from brewing, it would not do so before he endured some difficult family problems.

It is important to know that the second Arthur Guinness was a man of deep faith. His father's unswerving piety took root in his soul, where it merged with an evangelical fire. We can hear this even at the end of his life, in a letter he addressed to his sons.

> The continued good account of our Business calls for much thankfulness to Almighty God while we humbly ask for the infinitely higher blessings of His Grace in the Lord Jesus Christ . . . Surely it becomes me to speak of the Lord's patience and longsuffering towards one so utterly evil and sinful and to pray that I might be enabled through Grace to live every hour under the teaching of the Holy Spirit patiently abiding His time for calling me to that Place [of] Everlasting Rest, the purchase of the precious blood of the Lamb of God for saved sinners.

This brand of faith was nurtured chiefly at Bethesda

Chapel, where Arthur and his family were often to be found on a Sunday morning. The fires of the Great Awakening were still sweeping through Ireland in the second Arthur's day, and he was a willing vessel of its message. His pastor, a man named Benjamin Matthias, was a bold preacher of revival and reform and wrote books with titles such as *An Inquiry into the Doctrines of the Reformation and of the United Church of England and Ireland, respecting the Ruin and Recovery of Mankind*. Clearly, Arthur liked his Christianity hard-edged and fiery, and this brand of faith did much to make him the man he was.

His evangelical beliefs sometimes set him at tension with his Church of Ireland family members. We should remember that the Church of Ireland was essentially the Anglican church on Irish soil. It is understandable that members of the more staid, liturgical Irish church would feel themselves at odds with the boisterous, sometimes chaotic brand of evangelical revivalism practiced at Bethesda Chapel. It is also understandable that these lines of tension would reveal themselves even in a large and loving family like the Guinnesses.

Arthur's faith was more than mere emotion and religious sentimentalism, though, and nowhere is this more evident than in his care for the needy of his family. During his years at the helm of the brewery, he was beset with appeals for funds—from clergy relatives who could not support themselves, from other relatives whose investments had failed them, and from those relatives who could care for themselves but sought support for sons or daughters. It was nearly overwhelming. "I have from various causalities," Second Arthur wrote in response to one request, "which have, in the act of the Lord's providence, fallen out, chiefly affecting the property of my many dear Relations, had several individuals and families depending on me solely or partially for support . . . so that although the Lord has been pleased to prosper mine and my sons' industry, I have not been accumulating as you suppose, and indeed, I think I could not have done so acting as a Christian man." The truth was that he not only helped his relations from brewery funds but he answered many a request for help from his own pocket, including the repeated appeals from his irresponsible brother, Edward. Clearly, he saw it as his duty to care for his less fortunate family members, though at times he wished they would do more to care for themselves. "May I recommend, my dear Olivia," he wrote to his sister, "that you keep a systematic account of all your expenditure for in that way you may more easily judge." This was the gentle prodding of a successful older brother who knew that mismanagement was often at the heart of his family's woes.

Give generously though he might, Arthur still endured the wrath of family members who thought him unjust. It was painful; we can feel his anger and distress in one particular letter. It was written to Hosea, his older brother, who had dared to suggest that Arthur was not caring for Edward as he should.

My dear Hosea,

I feel myself placed in a painful and delicate situation when called upon to address my Elder Brother, and a brother who I do so sincerely love and respect upon the subject of his pecuniary concerns but my situation by which I am unavoidably obliged to act as the Family Banker forces me to speak plainly . . . What claim had Edward upon the Trade? Had he rendered any service to the Trade to entitle him to an annuity, and was it for a given period of years? Certainly not; upon what could he have founded "expectation of future advantage from continuance in the House." Surely upon nothing.

Fortunately, Arthur was a self-examining evangelical and did not allow offenses to take root in his heart. Instead, he sought to offer all of his pursuits to God. As he wrote to his son, Benjamin, "recollect that although diligence in our worldly calling is our indispensable duty as Christians, yet we have higher than these to engage our attention for we have a Heavenly calling in Christ Jesus and to this our supreme diligence is required." It was this "diligence in our worldly calling," which certainly included his management of the brewery, that allowed Arthur to take the firm to new heights. Though in 1821, still recovering from the depression, Guinness sold 30,519 barrels of porter; by 1828 that number had increased to 42,384. In a matter of years, the company would surpass every other brewer in Ireland in producing 68,357 barrels in one year. This was in 1833, and it has continued to be the largest ever since.

It is hard to know exactly why, around 1820, the second Arthur Guinness decided to leave his duties at the brewery and give himself completely to banking and finance. Perhaps he felt the brewery was on an upward course and could be tended by others. Perhaps he was weary of the constant carping about money within his own family and he wanted a break. Then, too, he may have been exhausted with the religious tensions that wracked not only his own family but his nation as a whole.

Though the Guinnesses were strong defenders of Catholic civil rights, they nevertheless came under vicious assault from the very people they sought to help. This was likely due to a forgery that occurred in 1812. In that year, radical antipapist groups sent petitions to the British government opposing concessions for Catholics. One of the petitions included the forged names of several Guinness family members. The second Arthur was so incensed that he offered a five-hundred-pound reward for anyone who could name the forger. The damage was done, though. Catholics grew suspicious despite the fact that even the local press insisted that signing such a petition was contrary to all that the Guinnesses had stood for. Embarrassed, the Catholic Board passed a resolution defending the Guinness family as entitled to the "confidence, gratitude and thanks of the Catholics of Ireland."

Radical Catholics weren't appeased. In October of

1813, a popular Catholic satirical journal printed this piece of verse attacking the head of the Guinness clan:

> To be sure did you hear
> Of the heresy beer
> That was made for to poison the Pope?
> To hide the man a sin is
> His name is Arthur Guinness
> For Salvation he never can hope.

The assault grew sillier still. Some Catholics were swayed by the claim of a Dr. Brennan, who insisted that Guinness beer had been "impregnated" with 136 thousand tons of Bibles and 501 thousand cartloads of hymnbooks and Protestant catechisms. He claimed that Guinness was an "anti-popery porter" that no good Catholic ought to consume. It was an attempt to damage Guinness sales more than it was a genuine assault on Protestantism, and it failed to achieve its aim.

Arthur Guinness II
(the Second Arthur)

Still, the Protestant–Catholic tensions wore at Arthur and he drifted ever further away from the firm and toward his banking and financial pursuits. Increasingly, his two younger sons, Arthur Lee and Benjamin Lee, ran the company in their father's frequent absences. His oldest son, William, had chosen the life of a clergyman, making him the second Guinness heir to the brewery to choose a life of religious service instead.

Now in his seventies, the second Arthur spent much of his time at Beaumont House, which he had purchased from his brother Hosea. During these years, he had the odd experience of having five unmarried daughters at home. Tending them and entertaining friends became his pastime. He sought a quieter life than he had known, enjoying his grandchildren and gently guiding his sons as they ran the brewery. Though as governor of the Bank of Ireland he had once hosted King George IV, Arthur came to eschew public life and he gradually soured on politics. When his son was asked to stand for Parliament, Arthur urged caution.

You will recollect that on two occasions a similar suggestion was conveyed to me, backed on both occasions by offers on the part of gentlemen who were candidates themselves and who offered to resign in my favor. I then felt, and now feel, that the office of sitting in Parliament of a great city and especially such a city as Dublin where party and sectarian strife so signally abound and more especially if filled by one engaged in our line of business, is fraught with difficulty and danger.

Yet, as much as the second Arthur may have sought a peaceful retirement, two events kept him from it. The first was the request of his son, Arthur Lee, to be released from his partnership in the brewery. This was a blow and the second Arthur grieved over his son's decision. It seems that Arthur Lee, the third Arthur, had not managed his affairs well and was hopelessly in debt. Moreover, he knew that he did not have the makings of a strong manager and that his interests lay elsewhere, in the arts and philosophy. Arthur Lee was devastated at the thought of injuring his father. A letter that survives reveals his torment.

My dear Father,

I well know it is impossible to justify to you my conduct if you will forgive me, it is much to ask, but I already feel you have and I will ever be sincerely grateful . . . I know not what I should say, but do my dear Father believe me I feel deeply . . . the extreme and undeserved kindness you have ever, and now, more than ever shown me.

Believe me above all that "for worlds" I would not hurt your mind, if I could avoid it—of all the living. Your feelings are most sacred to me, this situation, in which I have placed myself, has long caused me the acutest pain and your wishes on the subject must be religiously obeyed for me.

The second Arthur was moved by the plight of his son and chose to release him from his partnership in the firm and pay off his debts. His generosity allowed his son to buy a house just outside of Dublin. But the father could not have been pleased with how the son lived in the years that followed. Arthur Lee began drinking deeply from the mysticism of the ancient world. He collected paintings and composed pantheistic verse. He began to see himself as something of a Greek god and went about dressed to play the part. In truth, he became silly and effeminate. It was embarrassing, both to the family and to the aging second Arthur. His greatest concern, of course, was for his son's soul. He hoped for "some token of his being awakened to a sense of the value of the Gospel of the Lord Jesus and to an embracing of those invaluable truths." Such a token did not quickly appear.

The second Arthur's mind was soon distracted from the disappointing behavior of his son by the horrible potato blight that began to decimate Ireland. The potato crop of 1845 had failed, and famine—because a third of the population depended solely on the potato for food—spread quickly. The suffering was astonishing and hearts turned with hope to the next year's crop. But soon the black marks of the blight appeared again and the discerning knew that the plague of a generation had begun. Thousands upon thousands died horribly while governments vacillated. Rotting corpses clogged alleyways and filled the air with a nauseating stench. Tales circulated of mothers who murdered their children to spare them torment.

From his retirement, Arthur brought the matter to Benjamin Lee's attention. "How awful do the accounts from

Ireland continue," he wrote, "and how evident is it that the exertions of the Government need to be aided by those of private individuals." This was the good-hearted Arthur at his most naïve. He assumed, as many of his social class did, that the government was doing something. It wasn't. Then, in 1848, the blight struck again and the sufferings of the Irish were enough to drive men to madness. Thousands tried to leave the country, only to die on crowded boats. Hunger and disease beset hundreds of thousands more and now tales circulated of mothers who ate their children in the insanity of their starvation. Ireland became a hell of its own and the second Arthur tried to stir his son into action.

> In the *London Record* of last evening there is a letter from a correspondent who had been visiting Connemara and was just returned to another part of Galway, presenting a picture of the state of the destitution in Connemara exceeding in horror and misery anything we have before observed. May the Lord in his infinite mercy direct our Government and all individuals also possessing means to do so to the use of measures to relieve if possible the sufferings of our wretched poor people. I wish to know of any mode in which we might be able to aid in the work. You know my dear Ben that my purse is open to the call.

From his perch atop the Guinness brewery in Dublin, Benjamin Lee had trouble understanding the scope of the crisis. In time, he did respond, though, and both the family and the brewery gave generously to save lives. Oddly, it was the foppish Arthur Lee who led the way. From his home outside of Dublin—where he was nearer the more grievous suffering of the rural areas—he went to great lengths to help the peasants in his region and to care for those who served on his estate. Families heading for certain death survived as a result. So grateful were his workers that they erected a small obelisk made of Connemara marble in his honor and engraved it with these words:

1847
TO ARTHUR LEE GUINNESS ESQ
STILLORGAN PARK

To mark the veneration of his faithful labourers
who in a period of dire distress were protected by
his generous liberality from the prevailing destitution.

This humble testimonial is respectfully
dedicated consisting of home material.

Its colour serves to remind that the memory of
benefits will ever remain green in Irish hearts.

It is satisfying to know that not only was the second Arthur Guinness allowed to play a role in alleviating his nation's suffering, but also that from old age he looked out on a life, a family, and a brewery that moved him to prayerful gratitude. "My bodily health and my mental vigour are both preserved to a degree very unusual at the age of nearly 84," he wrote. "Every step of my protracted journey has been marked on the part of my God with Mercy." Then, too, there was the success of the many charities he served, from an organization designed to improve the lot of chimney sweeps to the Farming Society of Ireland to the cause of Meath Hospital, which his father had also served. For these and other services to his people, the *Freeman's Journal* called him "our most distinguished citizen." Writing to Benjamin Lee, thankful that the brewery under his son's leadership prospered more than ever, Arthur wrote, "We have much cause for continued thanksgiving to our God 'who giveth us all things richly to possess.'"

The second Arthur died in June of 1855 at the age of 87. His was a good life, lived for the glory of his God and to extend the legacy of his family to future generations. Understanding that he lived for a purpose beyond this world, the people of Dublin honored him with this elegy.

> Now Dublin City's into mourning thrown,
> Its leading member to the grave is cast!
> Is gone—for ever fled—
> This honor'd man is dead—
> Of rich and poor throughout the land
> Fam'd Guinness was the pride.
> Dead—no—he lives on some more glorious shore,
> He lives—but ah! he lives to us no more.

With his father dead and his brother, Arthur Lee, out of the business, Benjamin Lee took the reins of the Guinness brewery in a typically bold and energetic manner. He had begun as an apprentice when he was sixteen years old. Six years later, he had made partner. His gifts were evident to everyone and it was widely known that while the second Arthur tended banking concerns, his son Benjamin had presided over the dramatic expansion of the firm after 1840.

Even before his father's death, he had distinguished himself outside the company. In 1851, he had been elected lord mayor of Dublin. His election was celebrated with a pomp that the first Arthur would not have approved. Still, Benjamin was cut from different cloth and lived in a different age. The second Arthur understood, though when his son declined to run for Parliament out of concern for his wife, Bessie's, ill health, the father was pleased and told his son he blessed God for "the measure of his Grace which has led you to this happy decision."

Benjamin stepped into the leadership of the firm with the confidence of a man stepping onto the stage of his destiny. His change of residence may be the best symbol of his intention to lead the company in a style of his own. He moved his family out of the residence at Number 1 Thomas Street, which was nearly across the street from the brewery, and he turned that building into offices. He then purchased a luxurious town home at 80 St. Stephen's Green in a fashionable Dublin neighborhood. Not long after, he bought the adjoining house, number 81, tore down the dividing wall between the two properties, and created a new and lavish mansion. It soon was headquarters for the brand of regal hospitality that marked a new generation of Guinnesses.

His leadership of the company was equally unique and transforming. As Derek Wilson has written in his invaluable *Dark and Light: The Story of the Guinness Family*, "The changes that occurred in the life of Benjamin Guinness and the brewery in the thirteen years between his father's death and his own merit the description 'revolutionary.'" He was determined to expand the reach of Guinness and expand it dramatically. He began by targeting foreign markets. Involving his cousins, Edward and John Burke, both excellent strategists, Benjamin created an international distribution agency that began marketing Guinness abroad. By 1860, Guinness was being sold as far away as Australia and South Africa.

Yet the most dramatic growth of the Guinness brand during Benjamin's years of leadership was at home in Ireland. Taking advantage of developments in railroad transportation and improvements in Ireland's canals, Benjamin engineered a 400 percent increase in market share within his homeland. This tightened connection to the homeland was symbolized by the decision to use the Irish harp as the Guinness emblem. This came in 1862 and would prove to be one of the most brilliant marketing decisions the company ever made.

The harp model for the Guinness symbol had long sat at Trinity College and was dearly treasured by the Irish people. Called Brian Bóraimhe's harp, it was the musical instrument associated with the legendary tenth-century High King of Ireland who delivered his land from the Danes. One historian has called the harp the "most revered inanimate object in Ireland." It is hard to describe the degree of national pride that this symbol inspired. Brian Bóraimhe (often anglicized to "Boru") was beloved among the Irish because, as later romantics recounted, it was "he that released the men of Erin [Ireland] and its women from the bondage and inequity of the foreigners." Guinness chose the symbol as its own at a time when interest in Gaelic arts was increasing around the world and when Irish national pride was emerging from the bruising it had sustained during potato famines and the departure of a million people for other lands. Now adorned by this symbol of Irish heritage and courage, Guinness sales soared at home and abroad, where many an expatriate Irishman drank Guinness as a patriotic act.

With Guinness markets expanding and with the company now an international symbol of Irish pride and ingenuity, Benjamin Lee thrived. He became the richest man in Ireland, was elected to Parliament, and purchased a home on Park Lane in London that became a center of gracious living and hospitality. His charming manner won many a friend among England's upper class. This was good for Ireland, good for Guinness, and, of course, good for Benjamin Lee: he would become the first Guinness to receive a knighthood.

The esteem in which he was held is captured in a book from the time, titled *Fortunes Made in Business Or Life Struggles of Successful People*. Its author is anonymous but it was written with the purpose of many a book in that thriving industrial age—to inspire personal achievement in a time of unprecedented opportunity. Men as diverse as Carnegie and Krupp, Rothschild and Rockefeller, are described in its pages, all with an eye to distilling the characteristics of greatness and success.

In the airy phrases of that time, the book proclaims that "Benjamin Lee Guinness was in full control of an undertaking that under his energetic guidance promised to reach proportions that the original founder of the business could never have dreamt of." The decision to market abroad, for example, was due to the fact that Benjamin "had carefully thought out the whole matter before embarking upon so serious a change in the policy and traditions of the firm, and in order to adapt the Guinness product to the conditions of an export trade, and to the somewhat different taste prevailing in other countries, introduced fresh varieties of porter solely for purpose of export."

The resulting success forced expansion at the plant, of which—according to the book—Benjamin Lee was master: "He erected new buildings for making and storing malt and hops, introduced vessels of such huge proportions as had never before been seen for mashing purposes, provided an entirely fresh supply of water, had immense new boilers put in for heating, also gigantic fermenting tuns, coolers of fabulous capacity, and a number of other machines, making together such an assemblage of brewing plant as could be seen elsewhere."

Probably correctly, the book attributes much of the astonishing success of Guinness in Benjamin Lee's years to his personal style of management. The description that follows is not only typical of portrayals of Benjamin Lee from the time but is also filled with just the type of insight into business genius that readers of Benjamin Lee's time were looking for.

Early and late he was to be seen at the brewery, not simply delegating the various duties of management to others, but taking upon himself more or less the responsibilities of every department, and watching the daily course of business at every point. Not that he did not impose adequate responsibilities upon others; for this he did, and was as fortunate in his selection of men for the chief positions as he was in perceiving the various necessities of adaptability which an increasing trade involved.

He was no hard taskmaster, however, for he believed in ruling by kindness rather than sternness, knowing full well that the way to get the best service out of a man is to let him feel that he is appreciated and cared for. It is said of him that there was not a workman connected with the brewery, no matter how humbled his duties were, that he did not know and maintain friendly relations with.

Concluding its tribute to the "Great Man of Guinness," the book celebrated Benjamin Lee's character and the high esteem in which the Irish people held him:

He occupied a position of unique distinction in Dublin. He was not only recognized as the most eminent man of business at the time connected with the city of his birth, but he was also a man of large public spirit, to whom doing good to his fellow men was a pleasure— one almost might say a passion—and in the service he so willingly rendered to the public he was not less devoted and enthusiastic than in the conduct of his colossal business. He was thorough in everything and always cherished noble ideas of life and conduct. No wonder that such a man should have won the affection and esteem of those amongst whom he lived and that the highest honours within the power of the people of Dublin to bestow should have been tendered to him.

Yet while Benjamin Lee was highly regarded for his astonishingly successful leadership of the family firm, it was his decision to fund and oversee the restoration of St. Patrick's Cathedral that has caused him to live with affection in Irish memory. Founded in 1192, the cathedral was the shining historic symbol of Christianity in Ireland. It was associated with much that Irish Christians viewed with pride: that it was built on the site where St. Patrick first baptized new believers, that Jonathan Swift had been dean

Photo by Isaac Darnall

A view of St. Patrick's Cathedral (Church of Ireland) from the
gardens created during the second Guinness renovation

there in the 1700s, that the first performance of Handel's
Messiah had taken place there, and yes, even that the first
Arthur Guinness had made the cathedral his spiritual
home. Yet by 1860, the venerable church had fallen into
such horrible decline that many feared the structure might
completely collapse.

Benjamin Lee Guinness decided to intervene. For many
who knew him, it was a surprising decision. As Michele
Guinness has written, "Although *Spes Mea in Deo* ('My
Hope is in God') was the family motto, Benjamin Lee's
trust in a gospel of self-help often appeared greater than

his trust in God." He maintained a loose spirituality, preferring the more formal Irish national church to the evangelical Christianity centered at Bethesda Chapel that his wife, Bessie, embraced. Indeed, she grew in time to fear for her husband's soul. Ill for many years and contemplating her death and what it might mean for her husband, Bessie wrote of her concern for Benjamin to one of her sons.

Do my darling avoid bad company, I mean worldlings, for there will be plenty anxious to come here, and do guard darling papa from designing worldly women, for he will be much set on and might easily be taken in. I do not mean that he should not marry, but that he should get one who would help him on to that future world and not lead him to think of or live for the present.

Still, whether from a depth of piety his family did not know or from more patriotic sentiments, Benjamin Lee threw himself into the task of restoring St. Patrick's. He gave just over £150,000 to the cause, a massive sum for the day, equal to nearly $4,000,000 now. And he directed the work himself. It would take five years and much of his time, but the results live on as testament to both Irish Christianity and Guinness generosity. As the anonymous author of *Fortunes Made in Business* wrote, "He employed the highest architectural skill of the time in the work, and when, in 1865, the restored building was re-opened, with more than its ancient grandeur given back to it, it was felt that the restorer (Benjamin), who had personally superintended the carrying out of the work as diligently as he was accustomed to look after the affairs of his brewery, had done a memorable thing."

Photo by Isaac Darnall

When Benjamin Lee Guinness died in London on May 19, 1868, obituaries proclaimed that he had permanently transformed the Guinness firm. It was true. He had tripled

The author in the Guinness family pew at St. Patrick's Cathedral, Dublin

the acreage covered by the plant, making it one of the largest breweries in the world. He had dramatically increased Guinness markets both at home and abroad and in the process he had become the richest man in the land, leaving behind an enormous personal fortune of more than £1,100,000 upon his death. Perhaps the most startling tribute to his leadership became evident some years later, when corporate reports revealed that between 1837 and 1887, Guinness sales had increased thirtyfold. Much of this was due to the astuteness and industry of Benjamin Lee Guinness.

Yet another of his most ingenious decisions became evident after his death. He had expressed in his will that he hoped his sons would continue to serve "at the same place by their Ancestors for so many years." He had two sons, Arthur Edward and Edward Cecil, both of whom had apprenticed at the brewery. Yet by the time of his father's death, Arthur Edward began turning away from the brewery to pursue a life in politics. He was elected to Parliament, found it more to his liking, and within a decade of his father's passing, he asked his brother to buy him out.

Benjamin Lee had anticipated such a possibility. In his

Window honoring the Guinness family in St. Patrick's Cathedral

Statue of Benjamin Guinness near the
south entrance of St. Patrick's Cathedral

will he had directed that "Brewery concerns shall not be divided or broken up but shall remain as they now are." His wish was that the son who chose to leave the family business should sell to "his brother so continuing in said business and to no other persona whatsoever." This is exactly what occurred. In 1876, Arthur Edward formally withdrew from the brewery, selling his half interest to Edward Cecil for £600,000. This resulted from the brilliant decision on the part of Benjamin Lee to assure that the firm stayed in family hands. As two Guinness historians later wrote, "He was typical of many Victorian Industrialists, but more far-seeing than most, in his awareness of the temptations which great wealth offered the next generation."

After Benjamin Lee's death in 1868, his son Edward Cecil then became head of the company, for eight years as partner to his brother, Arthur, and then alone after Arthur sold his interest in the company to pursue a political career. The Edward Cecil years would be a time of dramatic prosperity. He had received from his father a brewery that was the largest in Ireland and one of the half dozen largest in the world. Before he had finished leaving his imprint on the family firm, Edward Cecil would make Guinness into the largest and most successful brewery ever known. Even the statistics from the early years are astonishing. During the eight years that Edward and Arthur led the company as partners, the annual output of 350,411 in 1868 doubled to 778,597 barrels in 1876. From that time on, annual output increased 5 percent annually, surpassing 1.2 million barrels by 1886.

Edward Cecil was a different man from his father.

Though both enjoyed wealth and knew the gentlemanly arts of sport and pleasure, Edward ran the firm in a less hands-on fashion than Benjamin Lee. As we have seen, Edward's father was an ever-present, energetic man who was a familiar face to even the lowest tier of workers at the Guinness plant. He was personable, easy to converse with, and interested in each worker's responsibilities. His transformation of the company during his time as proprietor came from wisdom gained through observation, experience, and on-site management. His son, Edward Cecil, was a different kind of man. He was raised in startling wealth and had learned to love the life of the privileged. Though he would lead the company to new heights, he would do so through delegating authority to exceedingly capable men.

It was a management style fit for the age. It is difficult to express the pace of change that a man of Edward Cecil's time would have known, but perhaps one illustration will do. To use an American example, the American Civil War was fought from 1861 to 1865 largely utilizing rifles, cavalry charges, cannon, and strategies little different from those of the American Revolution nearly eighty years before. Less than fifty years later, the First World War was fought with machine guns, hand grenades, airplanes, submarines, radar, mustard gas, and tanks. The technological innovations during the years between these two wars, the time of Edward Cecil's reign over Guinness, was mind-boggling. An approach to management that relied on trusted experts and delegation served many a corporation of that time well, and Guinness perhaps most of all.

Edward was born in 1847 and was educated at Trinity College Dublin, where he earned his MA and LLD degrees. His devil-may-care attitude led some to believe he was a dandy, a wastrel of the upper class. But he was smarter than he at first appeared and, typical of his age of manhood, practiced the art of seeming more cavalier about life than he actually was. In truth, he was a quick study, a man keenly in tune with his times, and a deeply ambitious soul, eager to fulfill every potential of his wealth and privilege.

Though the brewery prospered while Edward was partnered with Arthur, this was nothing compared with the prosperity that came in the decade after. Edward saw to the

By permission of Irish Heritage Giftware; www.irishhistoricalpics.ie

Trinity College, 1890

construction of new offices and storage facilities of hops and grain. He also approved construction of brewhouse number 2 at St. James's Gate, a colossal structure that housed four mash tuns and would soon after be increased to eight. Having inherited his father's farsightedness, he realized how traffic on the River Liffey was increasing both in volume and in importance to his firm, so he bought a vast tract of land that lay between the brewery and the river, granting the company access to quays and thus to the Port of Dublin. To exploit this new access, in 1877 he contracted for a fleet of barges that would become enduring symbols of Guinness's strategic reach to the waterways of Ireland.

This dizzying season of expansion is summarized well in notes from a later head brewer, D. Owen Williams:

The expansion of trade during the 1800's continued to leave Guinness short of plant and buildings to contain it. Between 1870 and 1876 the Brewhouse was mostly reconstructed. A new building containing bins, elevators, mills, and hoppers, necessary for the receipt and storage of malt and preparing it for brewing, was erected. The four existing kieves were increased to eight in 1865. The additional plant required for brewing and fermentation was also correspondingly increased, including the addition of new tuns and skimmers and five new vathouses, containing 72 vats, making a total of 134 vats. Most of this expansion was done in existing premises but the space available was already too small. By 1872, new ground had been acquired to the south of the main brewery east of Robert Street and new stables and an additional vathouse, No. 8, containing 32 vats, erected there. A large tract of land to the North between James's Street and the Liffey was bought in 1873, almost doubling the area of the brewery, and by 1874 a large maltings, a new cooperate, and new cask cleansing and racking sheds were being erected there. The new arrangements set the pattern that was to last for over a hundred years whereby the beer was brewed and fermented around the original premises to the south of James's Street and racked and dispatched to the north.

So great was the pace of growth at the Guinness brewery that necessity became the mother of invention. Realizing that expansion required more rapid transportation within the plant, Edward Cecil decided that the firm needed its own customized railroad, and—in a move typical of his management style—he entrusted the project to chief engineer Sam Geoghegan.

It was good that Geoghegan was one of the great engineering minds of his time, for his task was not an easy one. The challenge was to design a system that was of the right size to move amongst the Guinness buildings and yet could interchange with the standard-gauge track of the Great Southern & Western Railway at Kingsbridge Station, just adjacent to the new property Edward had acquired.

Geoghegan proposed a plan that used two tracks, a twenty-two–inch narrow-gauge system and a standard gauge that linked Guinness to the broader Irish rail. It was a brilliant solution and soon became a model for similar plants around the world.

Then Geoghegan had to solve another problem: the fifty-foot incline from the Liffey to the highest elevations of the Guinness plant. How could railroad cars make such an ascent? Some suggested elevators, but this plan was soon rejected as too time-consuming. The pace of the Guinness plant wouldn't allow for trains to wait for elevators that were slow and of limited capacity. Instead, Geoghegan decided to build an ingenious underground spiral tunnel that revolved two and a half times underneath James's Street, allowing train cars to move unimpeded from one end of the brewery to the other. A similar tunnel had been built under the Alps; Geoghegan knew of it and adapted the plan for use beneath the brewery. It was a remarkably original solution for the age. Geoghegan wasn't done, though. He added to his list of innovations a unique cooling system that eliminated dangerous carbon dioxide, which had long been a hazardous by-product of large-scale fermentation.

As brilliant as Geoghegan was in engineering creative solutions to Guinness challenges, Edward Cecil was his entrepreneurial match, and the world learned just how true this was in 1868 when he announced he was going to make Guinness a publicly traded company. It was another astounding Guinness innovation, once again copied by major brewers around the world.

In his ten years at the head of the firm, Edward Cecil had already grown the company by more than 56 percent. This was largely due to expanding foreign markets, to which Guinness was exporting over a million barrels of beer annually. In the eighteen years that Edward had been with Guinness, overall production had increased fourfold. Merging his own ambition with a gift for timing and the long-range view he inherited from his father, Edward decided it was the perfect moment to take the company public.

Personal considerations may have moved him to this decision as well. He was happily married to a renowned beauty named Adelaide, whom the family nicknamed Dodo for unknown but certainly kind reasons. Their marriage was notoriously fulfilling and produced three sons: Rupert Edward Cecil Lee Guinness, Arthur Ernest Guinness, and Walter Edward Guinness. Only Ernest involved himself in the family business, though, and this may have moved Edward Cecil to contemplate the Guinness generations to come and what their personal choices might mean for the well-being of the company. Moreover, he was somewhat distracted himself. He had been appointed Sheriff of Dublin and then later, when the Prince of Wales visited Ireland, was made High Sheriff. He was also made a baronet in the seat of Castleknock in County Dublin. Some six years later, he would be created first Baron Iveagh, of Iveagh, County Down, which was upgraded in succeeding years to a viscount and then an earl. This gave him the title of Lord Iveagh in the British peerage (County Down being then and still a part of the UK), thus elevating the Guinness name to dazzling heights. The first Arthur, who died an esteemed member of the Dublin upper-middle class, could hardly have envisioned it.

All of this may have informed his decision to make the family firm a public property. Whatever motivated him, it was one of the greatest stock offerings in British history. A stock prospectus issued by Baring on October 21, 1886, showed the offering as "250,000 ordinary shares at £10, another 250,000, 6 percent cumulative preferred shares at £10 and 150,000 5 percent debenture shares redeemable at the company's option in 20 years. One third of the ordinary shares were reserved for Edward Cecil, who became the Chairman of the new company to be known as Arthur Guinness, Son & Company, Limited." As the *Daily News* exulted, "Nothing within the memory of living man had been quite like it . . . On Saturday morning Baring's place was literally besieged. Special policemen kept back the pushing crowd of clerks, agents, messengers and City men, and pains were taken to have one of the swing doors only partly open, notwithstanding (or because of) whim one of the outer doors of Messrs. Baring's office was broken." Even the usually understated *Times of London* called the response "extraordinary."

On Monday, October 25, the stock offering sold out within an hour. Both the Irish and the English press strug-

Iveagh Trust building

gled to capture its import. Typical of Guinness generosity, workers at St. James's Gate received shares from Edward Cecil's portion and some employees even received cash bonuses. Edward Cecil Guinness was now the richest man in Ireland and one of the richest in the United Kingdom. Befitting his new station, he purchased a grand home at Grosvenor Place in London, furnished it lavishly, and made it a center of Irish culture and hospitality in the heart of England.

Yet as skilled as Edward Cecil was in expanding the family firm beyond anything his predecessors might have dreamed, it is not this that keeps his memory alive to this day. Indeed, as it is with many a great man of industry, it was not the creation of wealth but the benevolent use of wealth that framed his legacy for generations to come.

In 1889, Edward Cecil put £250,000 into the hands of three trustees to create the Guinness Trust, "to be held by them in trust for the creation of dwellings for the labouring poor" in Dublin and London. This proved to be one of the great acts of benevolence of his generation and it laid a foundation for the later Iveagh Trust, which continues to serve the needy of Ireland to this day. The *Times* described Edward's deed as "the most splendid act of private munificence that has been contemplated and carried out in our time by an Englishman." It was, indeed, an inspiring act of generosity and it helped alleviate suffering in both cities to an untold degree. Yet it was perfectly in keeping with the Guinness sense of social obligation, of the duty of the privileged to the less fortunate of society. It was a gift consistent with the faith and largesse of the Guinness generations that had come before, and it was predecessor to an equally thrilling investment in social problems, one that would change Ireland forever, as we shall see.

THE GOOD THAT
WEALTH CAN DO

I t is an old truism that a man is measured by the company he keeps. We believe this because we understand
that what surrounds a man, what he keeps near and
esteems as of value, is an extension of his inner life. This
includes his friends. The kind of people he is drawn to, the
brand of character he feels comfortable with, says much
about the man he truly is.

If this is so, then it must also be true that a company
should be measured by the culture it creates. Culture. It

means "what is encouraged to grow," the "behavior and ways of thinking that are inspired." Despite what a company's advertising may boast, aside from what mascot it adopts or the slogan it uses, it is what is inspired in the life of its people that is the most important indicator of how noble a venture that company may be.

This brings us to Guinness. In the minds of most of the people in the world, Guinness is beer and that is all there is to the story. But this is far from true. Guinness the beer is magnificent, yes, but it is the Guinness culture that for nearly two centuries changed the lives of Guinness workers, transformed poverty in Dublin, and inspired other companies to understand that care for their employees was their most important work. It was the Guinness culture of faith and kindness and generosity that moved men to seek out ways to serve their fellow men, to mend what the harshness of life had torn.

There is no better symbol of this culture than the efforts that Guinness inspired in Dublin in 1900, when the horrors of overcrowding, starvation, and disease were decimating thousands. It was then that a young doctor, a board of wise and kindhearted men, a hundred-year-old culture of benevolence, and one of the most searing crises in Ireland's history converged. And it became, in time, a triumph, a story men told their grandsons and executives repeated in boardrooms around the world. It was the moment when that noble Guinness culture spilled out of the brewery into the streets of a dying city. It was a time when Guinness demonstrated the good that righteous wealth can do.

A visitor to the Dublin of today finds a city that is a pleasant blend of European bustle, American marketing, and Irish grace. There are the soaring, ancient structures, of course: St. Patrick's and Christ Church and Dublin Castle, where a modern government serves beneath Norman towers. There is, also, the lapping River Liffey, the winding bloodstream of the city, which speaks of days gone by even as it frames streets adorned by Quicksilver, Donna Karan, and The Gap. And always there is the thrilling, maddening jumble of the people: the Irish natives, the immigrants from Eastern Europe, the expatriates from the States, the eager workers from Africa, and the youth from every European nation who study at Trinity College or who simply want to master English as the language of their future plans.

All seems vibrant and promising and sweet. So it is hard to imagine that there was a time—and not that long ago—when Dublin was the Calcutta of its day, a city so beset with filth and disease that its reputation tainted the good name of Irishmen wherever they went in the world.

But so it was. In the late 1800s, Dublin had become a cesspool, a bog of squalor, sickness, and vice. It not only had the highest rate of contagious disease but also the

Anglesea Market, Coles Lane, Dublin.

highest death rate of any city in Europe. Its citizens were pummeled with smallpox, measles, scarlet fever, typhus, whooping cough, diarrhea, dysentery, typhoid fever, and tuberculosis at a nearly unprecedented rate. While the upper classes fled to safer homes in England, the poor and the working classes were left to fend for themselves in a city the suffering of which reminds us of the most poverty-stricken regions of the Third World today.

Much of this misery was due to overcrowding. Ever since the famines of the 1840s, pressing hordes of immigrants had swarmed into Dublin in hopes of escaping their troubled lives elsewhere. Many intended to find a boat that could carry them to a more promising life on distant shores. Yet once they arrived in Dublin, they usually found that such a voyage was too expensive or that space on the few ships was limited or even that foreign ports were closed to the Irish for fear of pestilence and disease. Dublin, then, became a dammed-up city of the poor, the weak, and the unwell.

Conditions were more desperate than most outside of Ireland understood. One survey from the time showed that 33.9 percent of all families in Dublin lived in one-room dwellings. Sometimes, it was even worse. A medical officer in 1900 found that one house at No. 5 South Earle Street, designed as a single-family dwelling, was home instead to eleven families. This meant that as many as three to four dozen people shared a single toilet and a single water tap in the backyard. The potential for infection and even death from such conditions was greater than officials at first understood.

These agonies fell upon women and children most of all. As an observer from the time reported,

> The city was packed, especially with destitute women and children, widowed, orphaned, abandoned, or left behind as the menfolk sought work in England. The large number of soldiers barracked in Dublin, and the high proportion of Irish soldiers in the British Army, brought its own problems: numbers of women, both married and unmarried, and their children, were left to fend for themselves when the soldiers were moved on, or returned to Dublin on the death or desertion of their soldier husbands.

Ironically, much of the disease and misery that beset the lower classes was self-induced. Families routinely dumped waste and sewage into the River Liffey and then drew their drinking water from exactly the same place. This spread sickness at an exponential rate. Then there was the bedding. Most Irish families slept on straw that was rarely changed and was often covered only with dirty rags, both of which were nests for dangerous bacteria.

The revered Irish tradition of waking the dead played a role in spreading disease, as well. Routinely, the body of a deceased loved one would lay in the family home for as many as four nights. Meanwhile, the grieving family was expected to provide food, drink, and tobacco for huge crowds of visitors who milled about the dead body and thus exposed themselves to whatever disease had killed the deceased. Making matters worse, this tradition had the tragic side effect of spreading poverty, a condition in which disease thrives. As Tony Corcoran has written in his tender tribute, *The Goodness of Guinness,* "even for the poorest Dublin family, a four-horse hearse constituted a show of respectability to the community—despite the fact that the family had to borrow heavily from moneylenders to finance the show." Often, the grieving family could not repay their debts and so they would slide deeper into poverty and thus more deeply into the conditions in which disease and pestilence spread. Dublin was, as one historian has written, "a city of the damned." Few outside of Ireland cared about these conditions and those who did seldom had the ability to make any difference.

It was just as these matters were reaching their worst

that an exceptional man became the chief medical officer at the Guinness brewery. His name was Doctor John Lumsden, and it would be his energy, his compassion, and his scientific inquiry that would allow Guinness to change lives by the thousands in Dublin and to break new ground in the growing field of corporate social responsibility.

John Lumsden was, by all accounts, an extraordinary man. He was born on November 14, 1869, in Drogheda, County Louth, the only son in a family of five daughters. He attended medical school at the University of Dublin (Trinity College) and, after years in private practice and as a hospital physician, he came to Guinness a thirty-year-old doctor with radical ideas about public health care and the duty of corporations to the poor. That Guinness hired him at all shows its willingness to be stretched, to absorb ideas sometimes at odds with those that had guided its decisions in the past.

Lumsden joined Guinness in 1894 as its assistant chief medical officer and then later, in 1899, was promoted to chief medical officer. It was a role he was eager to assume, for he had been inspired in his vision of what a society could do for its poor by a man he deeply admired, a man who had been contending with poverty in Dublin for more than twenty years.

Dr. Charles Alexander Cameron was the Medical Officer of Health for the city of Dublin. Like Lumsden, he, too, was an exceptional man. Born in 1830, Cameron was the son of an army officer who had fought in what Americans call the War of 1812. Cameron's official biography calls it "the expedition against the United States in 1812." Although the senior Cameron was wounded eight times in this conflict, he loved the military life and wanted his son to follow him. But the younger Cameron knew early that medicine and public health were his fields, and he chose to attend Dublin School of Medicine for his training.

He would have a storied career, propelled as much by his groundbreaking articles on medical themes as by his devotion to public health. In 1862, he was elected public analyst for the city of Dublin. He became famous for enforcing a little-known measure, the Adulteration Act, and convicting more than fifty people of selling adulterated food. He was demonstrating what might be done to protect the health of Irishmen if their officials simply exercised the authority they already had.

In 1874, he became the co-medical officer of health in Dublin and then later held the post alone when his associate retired. Cameron was a whirlwind of reform. His efforts resulted in the closing of nearly two thousand habitations he designated unfit for human beings; he worked to assure drastic improvements to thousands more. He also used his literary skill to draw attention to the social crises of his day and, in particular, to press the matter of adequate housing for the poor into the public mind. For these and many other successes, he was knighted in 1885 for "his services in the cause of public health."

Yet what inspired a younger generation of activists like

Lumsden was Cameron's way of first understanding and then articulating the crisis at hand. Though a gentleman, a medical doctor, and, eventually, a knight of the realm, Cameron did not hesitate to actually enter the homes of the poor, to walk the streets of blighted neighborhoods. This gave him the firsthand perspective other health officials lacked. And it also allowed him to speak in tender personal terms about the plight of the poor. "During the 32 years that I have been the Chief Health Officer of Dublin," he once wrote, "I have seen much of the life amongst the poor and the very poor, and I have many remembrances of painful scenes that I have witnessed in their miserable homes." This was unusual for an official in the Victorian age, as was Cameron's respectful attitude toward the poor. Amazing his associates, who often showed a callous intolerance for the poverty-stricken, Cameron proclaimed, "I would like to bear testimony to the wonderful kindness which the poor show to those who are still poorer and more helpless than themselves." This not only challenged a popular conception of the poor as lazy and indifferent, but it also extolled to the surprised members of his own class the virtue Cameron had found among the poor. This was exactly what Charles Dickens had attempted to do in his novels, but it was an unexpected perspective coming from a man of Cameron's position.

As Lumsden devoured Cameron's writings, he would have read insightful analysis of Dublin's economy. Of the limited jobs available in the city, Cameron wrote, for example, "Dublin is not much of a manufacturing city. Its importance is due to being the centre of the Local Government of Ireland, the seat of the Superior Courts of Law, the headquarters of the Medical Profession, and the Banking and Insurance business, the seat of two Universities, and its large business as a port. There is comparatively less work for females in Dublin than in most English towns." Few thinkers in the field of public health had begun to perceive social ills in such a way, strategically linking a city's economy, employment potential, and demographics into a model for public health. Lumsden listened and learned.

He would have been moved, as well, by how Cameron could write of poverty in tender terms, of how he focused on the children as the most tortured victims of want:

Thousands of children go with naked feet even in winter. The want of warm clothing in winter often lays the foundation of future delicacy, and renders them less liable to resist the attacks of disease. The want of good food and warm clothing often causes the fatal sequelae to attacks of measles. Amongst the rich this disease is rarely fatal; but the children of the poor offer up many victims to it—not only so much during the attack, but in bronchial and other infections which supervene as consequences of neglect, insufficient clothing and nourishment. The Police-Aided Society for Providing Clothes for Poor Children performs good work in Dublin, and deserves more support than it receives from the general public.

This was compassion and scientific analysis blended in a way that was rare and certainly stirring to Lumsden, but it would be Cameron's conclusions about poverty in Dublin that would ignite the young firebrand most of all.

It is not in the power of the Sanitary Authorities to remove many of the evils from which the poor suffer. They cannot augment their deficient earnings: they can only employ a very small proportion of them as labourers in the various civic departments. They can, however, soften the hard conditions under which the poor, especially the very poor, exist. How? By providing them with homes superior to those they now have, without increasing their rents. The most urgent want of the labourers and the poorer tradesmen is better dwellings. This is a measure that should be carried out liberally.

Here, in the kind of tough-minded analysis that the crisis demanded, was the mandate for action men like Lumsden required. He wanted to serve the common good and use his skills to alleviate the suffering in his city. But how could he do it? People around him urged solutions that ranged from the sentimental and ineffective to the radical and impossible to achieve. Lumsden did not want to chase dreams: he wanted to make a difference. And Cameron showed him how. In the crammed slums of Dublin, housing was the key to public health. There was only so much officials could do about employment and pay, but housing and sanitary living? Here was a cause a brilliant young doctor could make his own.

Lumsden wasted little time once he became the chief medical officer at Guinness in 1899. Within a year, he decided he must do among the workers at Guinness and in the neighborhoods surrounding the brewery exactly what Cameron had done among the larger body of the poor in Dublin: enter their homes and learn of the situation for himself. His speed and intensity must have stunned the Guinness board. Writing them for permission to execute his plan, the young doctor explained, "It is with a deep sense of duty that I venture to bring under your notice the subject of tuberculosis, its prevention and treatment among your employees and their families." His intention, he told them, was to attempt to visit the home of every Guinness worker as soon as possible. He also wanted to enter as many as possible of the homes that surrounded the brewery grounds. It was a massive proposal—nearly three thousand people were employed by Guinness at the time and these would have represented thousands more family members. This meant hundreds and hundreds of homes had to be visited. And these numbers did not include the hundreds of non-Guinness homes near the brewery.

The proposal must have given the Guinness board pause. As experienced men in business who were used to thinking in terms of strategy and future planning, they could see what was coming. Dr. Lumsden did not plan this survey of homes simply to gather data. He was sure to return at the conclusion with ideas for change, with plans for ways that Guinness could spend money to alleviate suffering. They knew Dr. Lumsden was going to cost them—and cost them dearly.

And yet they approved the young doctor's plan. Perhaps it was because they knew the time for broader reform had come. Or perhaps they had wanted to make a greater difference in the suffering of their time but didn't know quite how. Then again, it may have simply been the persuasiveness of the young doctor. He had worked for them for more than five years and was beloved throughout the workforce. Since the infirmary he manned was in Thomas Court, right in the heart of the tenement houses, the workers knew him, trusted him, and held the capable young doctor in a regard that must have reached the ears of the board. All of this surely shaped their decision to support Lumsden's plan.

Typical of his profession, Lumsden prepared carefully. As he later reported, "a considerable time was taken up prior to the inspection in obtaining the necessary information from the various departments as to the correct addresses of the employees." The workers were informed, the staff was prepared, and the plan was launched.

The visitations began on November 17, 1900, and were concluded on January 17, 1901. Of these approximately 60 days, Lumsden visited homes on 48 of them, often working Saturdays and always forced to work only during daylight hours, since the homes did not have electricity.

He averaged 36.5 homes a day. By the time he was done, he had visited 1,752 residences, which represented some 2,287 employees. These employees, in turn, represented more than 7,343 dependents.

Interestingly, only one worker refused to allow Lumsden into his home and, though this was an amazing success rate, the slightly miffed doctor included the almost humorous incident in his final report: "In only one instance did I fail to gain admission to a house, viz., that of a gate porter, who holds strong socialist views—a flat refusal of admission being given to me—not from any personal motive but on the grounds of principle. He held that it was no business of an employer how or where his servant lived. I wasted no words on him, but passed on to the next."

Lumsden's analysis of workers' houses was less amusing, though. He found that nearly 35 percent of the homes he visited were inadequate for use. His descriptions are wrenching. The houses, he wrote to the board, "are dens of disease . . . so impregnated with filth and so utterly rotten that they should be regarded as unfit for human habitation." In the depictions of squalor that follow he described solid excrement soiling stairways, sickening stench, the inadequacy of water supply, alcoholism, and rooms so vile he could hardly enter. The phrases that fall from Lumsden's pen are vivid and laced with anger: "squalid, miserable and unhealthy," "dirty personal habits," "bad management," "unworthy," "fever nests."

In his eagerness to make his point, the spirited doctor at

times risked being more vivid than the Guinness board was probably used to. Writing of the "lavatory arrangements" and in particular of the Earl Street area where there were often six toilets for as many as forty-five families, Lumsden wrote: "The females do not use these closets, I was informed, but instead use buckets which they empty into the dustbins. This is a truly shocking state of affairs . . . The actual closets are deplorable and appallingly filthy . . . the seats often made of common half-inch unplaned deal, put together in the roughest manner. In many cases I found them choked up to six or eight inches above the seat with sold human excrement!"

Yet as enraged as Lumsden became, he was not critical of the people who lived in these squalid tenements, as some health officials had been throughout the years. Adopting the manner of his mentor, Dr. Cameron, in describing the problem of alcoholism, Lumsden dared to confess, "For my part, I have always sympathized with the working man in his social surroundings; he has few opportunities of relaxation or enjoyment outside of the club or public house." This was a daring admission in an age savaged by alcohol abuse, but Lumsden was revealing the compassion that fueled his labors.

There was, too, some good news amidst this sad report: Lumsden found that the Guinness homes were vastly superior to the non-Guinness homes he surveyed. "These houses," he recounted to the board, "were all clean, tidy and home-like, many of them I am extremely pleased to be able to state were scrupulously clean and, in every sense, a credit to the occupiers." It was a pleasant note in a torrent of bad news.

Finally, Lumsden's conclusion was to the point: "I consider the conditions under which most of your people live, move and have their being is anything but satisfactory and far from what one would desire." His proposal for change was equally straightforward.

> If the firm could only see their way to erect more tenement buildings . . . I am convinced our people would flock to them from the wretched buildings . . . the mortality returns would be diminished, great contentment and happiness made possible, less sickness, want and misery would be evident . . . The moral effect of the inspection has been productive of much good . . . it has shown the people the interest the firm takes in their welfare.

In addition to this primary recommendation, Lumsden proposed six other courses of action that he believed would help in the short term. First, he suggested that the firm appoint an inspector of dwellings. His survey had done much good, not only in the gathering of facts but also in building goodwill with workers, and he believed the work should continue. Second, he surprisingly recommended that aid such as sick pay be withheld from workers who insisted upon living in dwellings condemned by the company. In other words, stop rewarding decisions that led to ill health. Third, he urged the company to keep a register of suitable housing, so that workers could be directed to better dwellings. Fourth, he wanted the company to exercise its considerable influence to keep its laborers from living in unhealthy tenements. Fifth, he suggested cooking classes be offered to women, the first of a flurry of recommendations he would make in regards to education. And finally, he recommended that "annual certificates of merit" be awarded to houses that were kept in good order. He would recommend more such awards in time, and they would go far in motivating families to improve their homes and themselves.

Yet of all that Dr. Lumsden reflected in his report, it may have been his contagious sense of mission and of the possibilities at hand that most won the board. The young doctor had reported some horrible conditions, yes, and in the most stark terms. But he was equally convinced that genuine changes could be made, that the situation was not so fixed as to be incapable of improvement. Much of this confidence arose from Dr. Lumsden's view of the Guinness workers themselves, from their innate goodness and willingness to improve if only they were shown how. As he wrote in a later report,

I personally have always found the majority of our men and their wives reasonable, intelligent and anxious to learn. They have to be tactfully handled and kindly treated, but they are always respectful, apparently grateful and often quick in appreciating the necessity for improvement. There are, of course, many infirmities of national character which time and education can alone overcome, but I am sanguine of the results, and I believe our people are capable of improvement, and worthy of the effort.

This positive spirit surely touched the Guinness board as they met to consider Dr. Lumsden's proposals on April 4, 1901. Judging by the portions of the board's minutes we have today, Dr. Lumsden's proposals were examined carefully.

Pending the erection of the Corporation's houses on the Bride Street area and the erection of Lord Iveagh's houses on the Bill Alley area, the only practical suggestion would seem to be that Mr. Busby (Registry Department) should place himself in touch with the existing agencies for the letting of houses.

Average number of families using the one WC. Dr. Lumsden to submit a draft letter to the Public Health Authorities with a view of urging them to take steps in this connection.

Cases of members of the opposite sex occupying the same sleeping apartment. [Particular case mentioned.] Dr. Lumsden will ascertain whether this case still exists, and if so will communicate with the Parish Priest.

This last point for the board's consideration arose from Dr. Lumsden's reporting that unmarried adults of the opposite sex were sometimes living in the same quarters and, indeed, sometimes sleeping in the same bed. The good doctor was compassionate about these conditions, explaining that this was a "not-uncommon state of affairs in the Dublin slums, I regret to say." Still, Lumsden was a devoted Christian and a deeply ethical man, so it was more than narrow Victorian values that moved him to thunder in his report, "This overcrowding, besides being unhealthy in the extreme and a means of the spread of disease, is also highly immoral." The board took the point, decided to check into the matter, and it is revealing of their broadmindedness that they determined to involve the local Catholic priest in solving this particular problem.

It is a tribute to the enduring benevolence of the Guinness firm that the board that convened in 1901 was eager to follow Dr. Lumsden's suggestions. It might have been otherwise. These senior men, some of them Guinness heirs, might well have felt themselves bullied and manipulated by this upstart, this fresh-faced young doctor with his novel ideas of corporate duties to the poor. They might have simply labeled him a radical or a socialist and ignored his suggestions or, worse, sent him away to ply his trade elsewhere. They might, too, have felt they had already done enough. Didn't they pay the highest wages possible? Wasn't their firm already the best place in Ireland to work? Hadn't they already brought employment and training to thousands? Why should they feel a responsibility to do more? This might well have been their response and few of the time would have blamed them had it been so.

Instead, they threw themselves into the vision Lumsden had set. They immediately approved funds for the certificates and contests the doctor recommended. They also agreed to keep registers of quality housing, to dispatch health officials to Guinness workers' homes, and to withhold aid from employees who stubbornly insisted on living in inadequate housing when better dwellings were available.

As important, notes from the board's meeting in October of 1901 reveal that brewery managers were dispatched to meet with employees whose homes did not meet Lumsden's standards for health. Reports from these meetings were studied by the board and from them we get a picture of the kinds of problems that plagued Guinness workers at the time. Some of the workers were surprised at Lumsden's evaluation, thought that their homes were adequate, but accepted responsibility for improving conditions according to the doctor's standards. Other men pointed to wives of "bad character" who would not do as they were told or as the company expected of employee spouses. Yet another man explained that his wife had been sick for many months but he promised that she was well now and that they would do all they could to answer the company's concerns. There were many other explanations and excuses, but what we should not forget is the image of board members from the largest brewery in the world examining in detail the reports of conditions in workers'

The Iveagh Market—Dublin's first indoor market—
was a local fixture for decades

homes. That the company hired a man like Lumsden in the first place, accepted his recommendations, and then spent so many hours working to improve conditions as he directed, is a moving statement of how much Guinness wanted to fulfill its legacy of compassion and generosity.

What the board likely did not understand at the time was where Lumsden hoped to lead them. He was aware of emerging trends in public health and he was watching, too, other thriving companies and how they cared for their employees. A hint at what he hoped Guinness might become appears at the end of a report he submitted to the board not long after his survey of homes. He first offered nine suggestions for improving workers' lives and all nine were eventually followed, as we shall see. Dr. Lumsden recommended that the company provide:

1. Technical education for the younger generation
2. Popular lectures of educational value
3. A program of athletics and exercise
4. Literature encouraging hygiene and the prevention of disease
5. Courses in cooking for mothers and young women
6. Education regarding the feeding of infants
7. Recreational opportunities in the form of concerts or socials
8. Opportunities for management and laborers to meet and socialize
9. Housing

It was while explaining, once again, this last point of housing that Dr. Lumsden tipped his hand.

Until our families are given the opportunity of being comfortably and decently housed, we cannot expect to do much in raising their social and moral standard. I therefore make so bold as to look forward to the day when a

Brewery Model Village is built on the lines of Cadbury's at Bournville [sic], and Lever Brothers at Port Sunlight, where our people can obtain a small one- or two-storied cottage at reasonable rent.

If the board had not understood before, here was Lumsden's vision clearly spelled out. He was grateful for the chance to serve as the company's medical officer, to survey the homes and improve sanitation, and to try to make Guinness a healthy place to work. But he clearly hoped for more. He dreamed of a day when an entire model village might be built, one in which workers could own their own cottages and where healthy living would be encouraged. This was where Lumsden hoped to take Guinness; to understand this further, we have to know something of the examples of Cadbury's and Lever that guided his thinking.

John Cadbury, founder of the world's largest chocolate company, was born in Birmingham, England, in 1801. He came from a long line of devoted Quakers and, as wonderfully as this faith shaped the social values of the company he would one day found, it also caused him to be treated with prejudice and discrimination throughout his life. As a Quaker, he was not allowed to study law or medicine in the universities of his day. A military career was also not an option, since Quakers are historically pacifists. Like many of his faith, he turned to business and underwent an apprenticeship as a tea dealer in the Leeds of 1818.

In 1824, Cadbury opened a small grocery store at 93 Bull Street in Birmingham. Like any good merchant, he not only became familiar with the needs of his customers but also grew to understand the evils that plagued his society. He came to believe that alcohol was the scourge of his generation. As a Quaker he had always contended that consuming alcohol was immoral, but he became even more certain of this when he saw the rampant drunkenness of his age, leaving poverty and vice in its wake. He decided to provide an alternative. By 1831, he had determined to leave the grocery business and to begin manufacturing chocolate and cocoa. He had convinced himself that "drinking chocolate" could become an alternative to the gin and whiskey that were ravaging so many lives. Merging his business skills with his Quaker sense of social duty, Cadbury bought an old malt house on Crooked Lane and began making chocolate.

His businesses thrived. Before long, Cadbury's had moved to a large factory on Bridge Street and was one of the major industries of Birmingham. In 1879, George Cadbury, John's son, took the lead of the firm and soon showed that he was as committed to social reform as his father. Rather than building a larger factory in Birmingham as their company prospered, George and his younger brother, Richard, decided to move the firm out of the slum-ridden city to a farming region four miles to the south. There they built Bournville, a model industrial village in which wages were relatively high, working conditions were excellent, medical services were provided, and experiments with workers' committees proved a thrilling success.

Bournville became a model of community planning and corporate social concern that was emulated the world over. In the decades after its founding, the Cadburys hired architect William Alexander Harvey to design neighborhoods of Arts and Crafts–style houses that were celebrated for their beauty, efficiency, and the manner in which they improved workers' lives. The Cadburys also developed programs for encouraging outdoor sports, social events, education, and even spa life, centered around the natural mineral springs that graced the village property.

Though Bournville has now been incorporated into the city of Birmingham, it still exists as a distinct community of more than 7,800 homes on 1,000 acres and is still honored as a valiant effort to answer the ravages of the industrial age with faith, generosity, and compassion.

What is important for our purposes, though, is how the Bournville of the early 1900s must have contrasted with Dublin in the mind of Dr. John Lumsden. Bournville was by that time a lovely village of happy workers who lived healthy, meaningful lives—all because a successful company had decided to use its wealth for social good. Lumsden's Dublin, though, was the European center of sickness and death. Lumsden wanted Guinness to bring this curse to an end. What he wanted was a Dublin version of Bournville, and when the young doctor visited Port Sunlight in 1905, this passion reached a fever pitch.

This model of corporate benevolence that completed Lumsden's inspiration was the vision of William Hesketh Lever. Born in 1851 in Bolton, England, Lever was educated at the Bolton Church Institute. He was trained for business in his father's grocery firm but in 1886, he decided to start a soap manufacturing company in partnership with his brother, James. Lever Brothers soap was the first that was manufactured using vegetable oils rather than animal fats. and this, combined with the Levers' production and marketing skills, lifted their new company to astounding success.

In 1888, Lever, now a fabulously wealthy man, decided to build a community similar to Cadbury's Bournville. Employing some thirty architects, Lever built his model village on fifty-six acres along the River Mersey. His goal was "to socialize and Christianise business relations and get back to that close family brotherhood that existed in the good old days of hand labor." Taking a bit more of a paternal approach than Cadbury's, Lever built Port Sunlight on a profit-sharing model in which Lever reinvested profits back into the village for his employees. As he explained this to workers, "It would not do you much good if you send it down your throats in the form of bottles of whiskey, bags of sweets, or fat geese at Christmas. On the other hand, if you leave the money with me, I shall use it to provide for you everything that makes life pleasant—nice houses, comfortable homes, and healthy recreation."

Lever worked to make Port Sunlight a worker's heaven. There were lovely homes in Old English, Dutch, and

Flemish architectural styles. There was a reproduction of Shakespeare's cottage at Stratford-On-Avon. Schools were built, parks were cultivated, and courses on nearly every skill, craft, and trade were provided. There were also an art gallery, a monthly publication, and a wide variety of athletic facilities. The village boasted several concert halls, one of which was so well planned that the Beatles performed there as late as 1962.

What men like Cadbury and Lever did to improve the conditions of their workers was replicated in other projects throughout England. There was Stewartby, originally built for the workers of the London Brick Company; the Woodlands, designed by Percy Bond Houfton; and Hampstead Garden Suburb, founded by Henrietta Barnett, to name but a few. Even when leading companies did not develop entire villages or planned communities, many still attempted dramatic efforts to improve the lives of their workers, largely because of the examples set by firms like Cadbury's and Lever. All of these were attempts to roll back the grinding poverty and crushing slum life that had risen to critical levels in the industrial age.

Lumsden toured both Bournville and Port Sunlight in 1905 and then went on to visit health facilities on the European continent. When he returned to Ireland, he submitted a report to the Guinness board. Typical of his well-known sense of humor, he called his report "A Summer Ramble." In it he described in glowing terms all that he had seen: the clean accommodations, the beautiful athletic facilities, the safe, wide streets, and the programs to encourage healthy living. It must have been a transforming time for the young doctor, now merely thirty-five years old, and it certainly clarified his vision not only for public health but also for his own life's work.

We do not have records that provide details, but it is obvious from the course of the next decades that Guinness did not wish to follow the examples of Cadbury and Lever. There would be nothing like the "Brewery Model Village" that Lumsden had proposed, no planned community a few miles outside of Dublin to serve as an example for the world. We can only speculate as to why. That it cannot be blamed on callousness of the Guinness board or a disregard for workers' lives seems clear given the company's long history of care for its employees. Historians have suggested many possible reasons, from the distractions of the oncoming war in Europe to a Guinness desire to find solutions right in the heart of Dublin where the monsters of want and poverty lived. All we can know for sure is that nothing of the Bournville or Port Sunlight kind of solution was ever attempted.

What Guinness did attempt to do, though, was to support its young medical officer, who was now aflame with a passion to transform lives tormented by the cruelties of the industrial age. In this, they may have received the better deal, for once John Lumsden understood that there would be no Guinness model community in the countryside of Ireland, he threw himself into the cause of making the Guinness brewery, at the heart of Dublin's urban center, a model of the caring, innovative corporate community.

Between his tour of resorts in 1905 and the onset of World War I, John Lumsden transformed himself into a one-man army of reform. To their credit, the Guinness board stood by him. There was nothing that touched the well-being of Guinness workers that the doctor did not make his concern. He started programs, lobbied for funds, lectured, cajoled, and wrote instructional material by the ream. As a result of his labors, Guinness gained a reputation for care of its employees that rivaled any other company in the world, and did so from the heart of Dublin, notorious as the most unsanitary and deadly city in Europe.

It is thrilling to look back on Lumsden's labors those years ago and to consider in how many matters he was ahead of his time. He was an early advocate of breast-feeding, for example, and worked hard, along with his staff, to teach women that breast milk was more nutritious than powdered milk formula and that breast-feeding also served as a natural—and church approved—form of birth control. To win victories for this cause, he lectured, wrote pamphlets, and urged his nurses to gently help new mothers make this practice their own.

He came to understand that many troubles arose from

bad financial management, so in 1903 he convinced a small group of workers' wives to keep diaries of their income and expenses. From this he learned not only where a typical worker's money went but also what the average family diet was, how alcohol impacted a husband's spending, and how the habits of generosity among Guinness workers were more pronounced than he thought.

All of this data allowed him to improve services to workers. Yet, like a good reformer, he also probed data from past eras at Guinness to understand the trends. One report he read, which dated from 1880, revealed that 44 percent of the deaths at the time were due to tuberculosis. Smallpox, typhus, and typhoid were also leading killers at that time. Dr. Lumsden may not have been surprised—as we certainly are—that the medication prescribed that year included 764 bottles of wine, 535 bottles of whiskey, and 213 bottles of brandy!

Armed with data from the past and the present, he was able to update Guinness's medical services. He hired well-trained staff, purchased the best equipment, and expanded the arena of his concerns well beyond tending the sick to assuring the conditions that made for healthy workers, whole families, and thriving, nurturing neighborhoods. In his wake he left athletic unions and playing fields, swimming pools and reading rooms, parks and awards for excellence for nearly every skill related to health, homemaking, and professional development.

Though nearly all of his efforts have had lasting results,

one of his projects in particular has touched many more lives through the years than he could have dreamed. As he began creating a healthier, safer environment at the brewery, he started teaching first-aid classes to Guinness workers. The brewery men loved these classes, as it gave them confidence in dealing with the wounds that routinely arose in their work. These classes were so popular, in fact, that these men later became the first registered division of the St. John Ambulance Brigade in Ireland. This connected Dr. Lumsden and St. James's Gate, as well as health care in Ireland, to the larger St. John Ambulance Association that had been founded in England in 1877 as a unifying organization for first aid and ambulance services.

The Irish Division of the St. John Ambulance played a storied role in many of Ireland's conflicts in the early twentieth century. During the general strike of 1913, the Easter Rising in 1916, and the Irish Civil War—conflicts Americans may know best from the movie *Michael Collins* starring Liam Neeson—members of Dr. Lumsden's brigade were a frequent sight, impartially tending the wounded from both sides of each violent episode and often saving lives with techniques that Lumsden had devised during his years at Guinness. In fact, many a soldier remembered that it was Dr. Lumsden himself whom they saw carrying a white flag in one hand and his medical bag in the other as he ran into the middle of a firefight to care for fallen men. Combatants learned to hold their fire as the esteemed doctor bandaged wounds and carried bleeding men from the field. It was an image that they seldom forgot, and made them believe—even in the heat of battle—that a better day might be possible for their troubled land. For this contribution and for his formation of the St. John Ambulance Society of Ireland, Dr. Lumsden was knighted by King George V, and seldom has the honor been as well deserved.

It is hard to exaggerate the good that John Lumsden accomplished in his life, both for Guinness and for Ireland as a whole. Yet some sense of his impact, both his and the benevolent culture of the Guinness clan, is evident in the life of a Dublin merchant today. His name is Malvin and he is in his sixties, but he remembers the story that has come down through his family line. It seems that his

Photo by Isaac Darnall

The Iveagh Play Centre opened in 1915 to provide after-school care and education for Dublin's poor. Approximately 900 children, ages three to fourteen, attended.

grandfather was working at the Guinness brewery one day in 1926 and happened to get his shoulder caught between two of the famous custom rail cars. The shoulder was horribly crushed and the blood spurting wildly indicated to nearby workers that the artery had been cut, usually an almost certain sign of death. But a few of the men looking on that day had listened closely when young Dr. Lumsden taught them first aid and they knew what to do. Knocking the panicked man to the ground, they stopped the bleeding, worked to prevent shock, and carried the man quickly to the infirmary, having bound the wound as they had been taught. And Malvin's grandfather lived. And he married. And he was able to tell his grandson this story years later as the two fished together off the pier at Howth.

There are thousands of stories like this and from them we get some sense of what Dr. Lumsden did. But we must remember that he could not have done it alone. He needed a culture of generosity and social concern from which to work. He needed wise men to stand with him and to take risks on his innovative ideas. And he needed an arena in which he was trusted, where he could work out the procedures and techniques that would save human lives. This, then, is what Guinness gave him. And this is one small example of the good that wealth can do.

THE GUINNESSES
FOR GOD

I have to confess that the title of this chapter bothers me and it isn't because it sounds too pious or because I'm afraid the God theme might turn the nonreligious away. No, it is because of a deeper theological issue, one that I think is critically important to what we believe about our lives in this world.

Historians of the Guinness saga tend to divide the family into three lines. There are the "brewing Guinnesses," of course, who are the best known due to their connection to the wildly popular global brand. There are also the "banking Guinnesses," who descend from Samuel Guinness, brother of the first Arthur, and have grown an empire that began with goldbeating in the 1700s and continues in global high finance today.

Then there is the line that Guinness historians tend to call the "Guinnesses for God." These descend from John Grattan Guinness, the youngest son of First Arthur, and continue through the centuries in lives so turned to God and so given to adventures of faith that, as Frederic Mullally has written in his thrilling *The Silver Salver: The Story of the Guinness Family*, they make the other Guinness lines "seem almost pedestrian."

It is true: the story of this deeply Christian line, of its missionaries and ministers who changed entire nations, is as delightful and challenging as any. Yet using the words *Guinnesses for God* seems to suggest that the other Guinnesses were somehow apart from God, or that perhaps they pursued far different gods from those worshipped by their relations. The banking Guinnesses are even called "Guinnesses for Gold" by some historians, as though they worshipped filthy lucre while their cousins sat piously in church. This is more than a matter of my preference for certain words: it is a theological matter that touches one of the great themes in the history of Christianity.

At the heart of the matter is whether work that is not specifically religious can be work done for the glory of God. Another equally important question is whether God calls men to trades and to vocations in this world as part of his unfolding plan or whether these common occupations are too mundane to be included in his will.

These are questions that theologians have grappled with throughout church history. The matter really comes down to how we determine what is holy: in other words, what in this world is set apart for God. In the early centuries of Christianity, the church was forced to continually define itself as distinct from pagan society and this established a simple line of division: the church, its ministers, and even its physical property were holy and everything else wasn't. This thinking continued into the late Middle Ages, but by then it became extreme. There was the world and there was the church and the two were seen as completely different and always at odds. So distinct was the church from the world that a man could literally step over a fence or a line drawn on the ground and find himself stepping from the holy to the profane. The problem became, though, that the daily lives of men were not considered part of the holy. They were part of the secular world, separated from the church and sometimes even from God. Daily work and family, laughter with friends, even the wonders of nature were viewed by many church leaders as separate from more lofty "heavenly things."

Reformation leaders like Luther and Calvin, writing in the 1500s, knew that this was not what scripture taught. They insisted, instead, that God called men not just to offices in the church but to every kind of labor and trade.

So in their thinking, the farmer was no less holy than the priest, the innkeeper no less ordained by God than the bishop. As Luther wrote, "What seem to be secular works are actually the praise of God and represent an obedience which is well-pleasing to him."

The Reformers also taught that while God did not want men to be worldly in character, he nevertheless called them to be active in the world in order to fulfill his will. So, rather than teaching, as the Roman Catholic Church did, that the further removed from society a man remained the more holy he was, the Reformers taught that holiness was a matter of conformity to the image of Jesus, which a man ought to exercise as openly in the world as possible. In other words, the Christian shopkeeper or candle maker served his God while he plied his trade as Jesus would—with skill, with excellence, with morality, and with joy. This would do more good in the world than a thousand monks hidden away in monasteries, so the Reformers believed. As Luther expressed in his usual blunt fashion, done to the glory of God, even "household chores are more to be valued than all the works of monks and nuns."

The Reformers, then, pulled down the artificial distinction between the sacred and the secular and sent men into the world to serve God by using their skills and trades in his honor. This Protestant ethos of work found its way into the lives of the Guinnesses through the deeply reformed faith of the first Arthur Guinness and certain of his descendants. Many of them understood that brewing could be done as a holy offering, as a craft yielded in the service of God. They did not see themselves as secular, but rather as called. They did not see themselves as apart from Christian ministry, but rather as in the Christian ministry of industry and trade. They did not think of their brewing work as a menial way to pay the bills, hoping that they might compensate for such worldliness by giving occasional service to the church. No, they had absorbed the great Reformation ideal that everything a man did was to be done for God and that his calling and his vocation were usually the same thing. They understood that this transformed workbenches into altars and the labor of a man's hands into liturgies pleasing to God.

So while I identify closely with the line of Guinnesses who were missionaries and ministers, I hesitate to think of them as any more connected to God than the other lines. A banker can be as called and as pleasing to God as Billy Graham may be when he preaches. A brewer can serve as valuable a role in the kingdom of God as a missionary, a priest, or a pope. This is the truth of Christianity and this, too, is a core truth of the Guinness story. It explains much of Guinness spirit; much of their success and the good that they have chosen to do in the world.

I have skipped over the tale of one of the first Arthur's children and I have done it on purpose so that we could capture the wonder of it here. It is the tale of John Grattan Guinness, the youngest son of First Arthur, the one that he and his wife, Olivia, probably worried about and prayed for the most.

Children are their own, unique creatures but they carry a piece of their parents with them in their souls. Together, all the children of a family reflect the sum of who their parents are, just as a prism reflects all the tones of the light; but each of them individually reflects only a part of the whole and this is often what makes each individual child such a fascinating extension of his or her parents' lives.

If this is so, John Grattan Guinness carried the wilder, more passionate side of First Arthur. Hosea, the oldest son and clergyman, would have reflected his father's faith. Second Arthur would have evidenced his father's steady hand, his managerial skill, and the wisdom that allowed him to lift a brewery to success. And so it would have been through the lives of all the children.

This tenth child, John Grattan, reflected the version of Arthur that we see in the story in which Arthur takes up a pickaxe and "with very much improper language" tells a sheriff he will not shut down his brewery's water supply. This is Arthur the fighter, Arthur the man fed up with bureaucrats and those who would stand in his way. This is the part of the Arthur spirit that filled John Grattan Guinness.

He was certainly the most strikingly handsome of Arthur's sons and this, as we know, often leads to trouble. But he was also reckless and adventurous, sometimes foolishly so. Perhaps he wearied of the staid lifestyle of his upper-class family. Perhaps he simply did not want his daunting father and doting brothers and sisters to tell him what to do. Or perhaps something more eternal struggled in his soul. Whatever the case, he seemed ever willing to crash out of the mold, to defy the family norm.

Born in 1783, by the age of fifteen he had already nearly been killed. When Catholic workers rose up in 1798 to establish an Irish Republic in imitation of the French revolutionaries, John wanted to join his brothers in putting the rebellion down. Told he was too young, he snuck away to fight anyway and was wounded on an errand to deliver secret dispatches.

What followed was the kind of clash of wills in which destinies are fashioned. Having tasted adventure, John declared that the brewer's life was not for him and that he intended to join the army. His father, Arthur, realizing he could not persuade the boy, was probably relieved. The army was a good life and not that unusual for the younger sons of wealthy men. Arthur must have put his hopes in what the army might do for his wildest child. We can almost hear him offering his son to God as the willful young man sailed off to join the English army in India.

John Grattan Guinness would spend his next years under the command of the legendary Irish soldier Arthur Wellesley, enforcing peace among the warring princely states in that torturously hot land. There were long weeks of pursuing rogue rajas across hundreds of miles of hostile territory. The fiery days and frozen nights wore a man down. As did fear. English soldiers who were caught had nails driven into their skulls or their necks wrung by Hindu strongmen known as Jetties. The British almost always prevailed, but the price to each man's health and spirit was dear.

John Grattan garrisoned at Seringapatam for many years and found that his greatest burden was not the enemy but the behavior of his fellow officers. Their drunken, quarreling, bullying ways were offensive to John, raised in refinement and Christian values as he was. He could not stomach the looting and the debauchery that the other officers allowed and this soon sent him into a season of soul-searching that would ultimately refocus his life.

Before this occurred, though, he was nearly ruined by his naïveté and his trust in his brothers in financial matters. His brother Edward contacted him about this time and told him of his plan to build a large ironworks at Palmerston and Lucan. But Edward did not have enough money and wondered if John might want to invest his inheritance— the £1,500 left to him in their father's will—in the plan. Edward promised that by the time John was in need of it, his money would have doubled, given the sure success of his plan.

Home on leave in 1810, John found a reason to claim his share. He had met Susanna Hutton, the daughter of a respected Dublin alderman, and decided to marry her. But he soon learned that Edward was just what his father had suspected: as foolish in matters of business as he was errant in matters of faith. The ironworks had failed and John's £1,500 were gone. It was a terrible blow. It meant that John had to take his new bride with him back to India and endure many more years of searing duty in that still unbroken land.

Yet it is often in discomfort that transitions of the soul are made, and this was true of John Grattan Guinness in the years that followed. Though in Ireland the evangelical message and its Wesleyan expressions were opposed and suppressed, in India many a fellow officer had absorbed this new type of faith and taken it to heart. John Grattan heard deep Christian truth from men he admired, men who chased their enemies with ferocity during the day and then prayed for a deeper love of Christ by their bedsides at night. As they shared their spiritual passions with Captain Guinness in the officers' mess, he was drawn in and soon reported in letters home that he had been "born again." India gave him time to grow in his new commitment and to deepen in it with his wife, Susanna, who became one with her husband in spiritual matters.

Despite the joys of their newfound faith, the years in India were difficult. The climate, the stress, and the dangers broke their health. He returned home in 1824, sick and exhausted. She returned with him but died two years later, though not before her husband was forced to endure a further humiliation from his brewery relations.

When John Grattan returned home, the second Arthur

felt obligated to put him to work. His younger brother had lost all of his inheritance, after all, and the successful head of the family brewery could not allow the now retired Captain Guinness to become destitute. Arthur sent his brother to Liverpool and told him to take over a Guinness agency at 29 Manesty Lane. With two partners, John was to operate an importing business that was separate from the family's other business concerns. His task was to import beer, but only as a sideline. The main import was Irish whiskey—and this is where the crisis arose. As an evangelical of his age, Captain Guinness was a teetotaler, a man who drank no alcohol and believed that all men should do likewise. Indeed, he had come to believe that whiskey was a source of evil, a cause of much of the wickedness that plagued the world. He tried to move the business away from beer and whiskey and toward bread and other products that would be healthy, even moral in his view. The scheme failed though. It was whiskey and beer that brought profits, not bread. In less than a year, John resigned from his position, sorry to have disappointed his brother but not wanting to make matters worse.

John Grattan might well have become a broken man during these days. He felt himself a failure in the army and a failure in business, as well. Then, too, his sons by Susanna, John Grattan (junior) and Arthur Grattan, had yet to prove themselves worthy. The younger John Grattan had even been fired from the brewery for "mixing with degraded company" and then failed to prove himself again after being given a second chance at a branch of the family firm in Bristol. It was a deep disappointment to Captain John, who added this episode to the list of failures that made him increasingly disillusioned about his life. He chose to retire in Cheltenham—"God's anteroom" for retired Indian Army officers—and took comfort at his Congregational church.

There was yet much to commend him, though. As Michele Guinness has written in *The Genius of Guinness*, the best book on the Grattan line,

> In middle age he was still the most handsome of the Guinness brothers, with an erect, military bearing and a strong, dignified face set off by the high collars and cravats he wore. There was no hint of grey in the dark hair, even in the long sideburns, and the only suggestion of the trauma of past years was the unusual pallor of his complexion. His youthful drive and bravado had long burnt out, leaving a shy man who often hid behind spectacles and preferred the simple, solitary pleasures of reading and walking to the high life of Dublin society.

We tend to forget that there are second acts possible in the lives of most men, that an unchangeable fixity does not always rule human affairs. Many a man who has come to late middle age with despair and disillusionment has found—perhaps in love or work or devotion to a cause—the meaning or fulfillment that eluded him earlier in life.

This was certainly the case with Captain John Guinness, who found his happiness in an elegant creature named Jane D'Esterre.

John Grattan Guinness and Jane Lucretia D'Esterre met at Dublin's York Street Chapel in 1829. He was a man in late middle age who was disappointed in his meager achievements, who contented himself in scripture reading and time alone. She was distractingly beautiful and it is not hard to understand how she captured the captain's heart. As Michele Guinness has described her,

Described in an early biography of O'Connell as "the beautiful Miss Cramer of Dublin," she looked, according to one of her sons, as if she had been "formed to

From the Archives of Michele Guinness

Jane Lucretia D'Esterre-Guinness

win admiration and affection . . . waving locks of dark hair falling over a high, fair forehead; the eyes dark brown and bright with intelligence; the eyebrows arched; the nose slightly aquiline; the mouth fairly large with mobile lips full of expression." She was indeed a beauty, and when she first appeared on the stage of the Theatre Royal, she took Dublin by storm, even catching the attention of the wild poet, Lord Byron.

Captain John Guinness

Yet by the time she met Captain Guinness she was also a woman with a complicated past. She had been married to John D'Esterre, a pork butcher known more for bluster than sense. He was a member of the Dublin Corporation (the organization that governed Dublin City) and when famed Catholic political leader Daniel O'Connell described the city fathers as "beggarly," D'Esterre took the slight personally and demanded satisfaction. Few took the matter seriously (including O'Connell at first), but D'Esterre would not let the matter die and so his challenge to a duel had to be accepted.

On February 2, 1815, the *Dublin Journal* reported the matter with stiff bias.

Yesterday, at four-o'clock in the evening, a meeting took place at Bishop's Court, between Mr. D'Esterre, one of the Representatives of the Guild of Merchants in the Common Council of Dublin, and Counselor O'Connell when we lament to say, the former was wounded in the hip. The cause of the quarrel was some insolent words used by Counselor O'Connell at one of the Popish Meetings, as against the Corporation of Dublin. These words Mr. D'Esterre resented, and desiring an explanation, was answered by further insolence, which induced him to press the meeting. Mr. D'Esterre's wound is considered dangerous: the ball has not been extracted.

The next day, D'Esterre died, leaving a widow—who knew nothing of the matter until her husband's body was carried into her house—and two small children.

She was an exceptional woman, though. Although she took a house in Ecclefechan in the lowlands of Scotland, the distance from Dublin did not distance her from her troubles. One day, as she sat by a river, she fought the temptation to plunge herself into the rushing waters. As the river called to her, she was awakened as from a dream by a plowboy whistling hymns. She watched the youth for a while and then felt convicted that she had sunk so far into self-pity while this simple man maintained such joy in the midst of his labors. She pulled herself together, decided she would not descend, and returned to Dublin to carve out a life as a music teacher. She also found faith in Jesus Christ as she heard a sermon at St. George's Church, a faith that was deep and transforming and restored her trust when so much trust had been broken in her life. She was still a very attractive woman who might have had an easier life had she acquiesced to any of the offers of marriage that came her way. But she kept herself apart, tended her family, and waited for the timing of her God.

That timing came when she met Captain Guinness. The two had known their disappointments and their pains, but their love became a salve for old wounds and a cause for a kind of hope neither of them had enjoyed in recent years. They lived primarily at Cheltenham, but also visited Dublin and Clifton with regularity. There were adult children to visit and relatives in the vast Guinness family to consult. In the first five years after their marriage in 1829, theirs was a happy but nomadic life.

Their story has meaning, if for no other reason than Captain John was the son of the founder of the Guinness clan and brewery. There is also the sheer drama of their lives and the vitality of the faith that saw them in good stead through their hardships. But there is another reason that their journeys are vital to the unfolding Guinness tale and it arrived in 1835. In that year, fifty-two-year-old Captain John Guinness and thirty-eight-year-old Jane D'Esterre Guinness had a son, whose name was Henry. Born in his parents' latter years—and regarded by them as a token of God's unceasing grace—Henry Grattan Guinness would become such a firebrand of faith in his time that his name would be mentioned with Dwight L. Moody and Charles Spurgeon as one of the greatest preachers of his age.

His first twenty years of life did not betray this promise, though. Henry grew up in a community of retired military men and heard often of thrilling adventures in exotic lands, of narrow escapes from strange and dangerous men. These tales worked on his young imagination, and by the time he turned fourteen—the same year his father died—he had come to regard the life of a brewer as far too dull compared to the life he hoped to live. He spent his days dreaming, roaming the woods, or climbing on nearby castle ruins. When he turned seventeen, he decided to follow his brother, Wyndham, and go to sea.

Already, though, the seeds of a powerful faith had been planted in his soul. He grew up in a deeply Christian family, with daily prayers, Sunday services, and charity work forming the pillars of life. Though his mind was often elsewhere during many of these devotional times, there was one occasion he recalled with tenderness all his life. His father had asked him to read a favorite passage from the book of Revelation and as Henry did, he remembered . . .

> the light of the street lamp shining in to the quiet room, where we sat together, and the solemn and beautiful imagery of the chapter relating to the New Jerusalem seeming to shed over the scene a purer and loftier light. Though but a child at the time, I think I entered more or less into my father's profound admiration for the passage, and felt with him the vibration of the soul attuned to eternal realities.

Despite these early stirrings, he went to sea in 1853 and "fell into evil company and evil ways." He returned home for a visit a year later and was delighted to find that his brother Wyndham was on leave too. Henry was eager to hear of Wyndham's exotic adventures, but instead heard how his brother found faith in Christ at the urging of a Christian chief mate named Peek. It was all that Wyndham wanted to talk about and the two brothers spoke into the morning hours one night of Jesus Christ and his will for men. Finally, Wyndham fell asleep, but Henry was too stirred of soul to rest. He later said that his brother had painted a "mental vision of moral loveliness such as I had never seen before." The next morning, the family began noticing that he was changed, that he read devotionals and spent time in prayer.

The process of transformation was begun but not complete. He went to sea again but became so ill that he was soon put ashore. While recuperating, he began to think about a different career and decided that farming might be just the thing. Soon he found a farmer near Cashel who would take him in and he set himself to learn the planter's life. Not long after, though, he was out shooting when he badly sprained his ankle. This led to days on his back while he healed and during this time he started contemplating his ways. He regretted his twenty years of aimlessness and began to search the Scriptures for something deeper to define his life. He found it. As he later wrote,

The future was lighted with hope. The gates of glory and immortality opened to my mental vision and there shone before me an interminable vista of pure and perfect existence in the life to come. It was the marriage of the soul; the union of the creature in appropriating and self-yielding love with Him who is uncreated eternal love.

He was a man afire. He returned to his mother's home in Cheltenham and joined her in evangelistic work. He also applied to New College London, in hopes of completing the studies a useful minister would need. But he did so with trepidation. He had already noted the "dampening effect" of formal learning on spiritual zeal and he later recounted how "with many tears I besought God on the night of my admission, walking the streets of the great city, to keep me from backsliding and growing cold about Divine things." Such concerns were not a basis for academic success and he did not finish his second year.

He did begin preaching, though, and at this he was an amazing success. On his twenty-first birthday he wrote in his diary that his only passion was "to live preaching and to die preaching; to live and die in the pulpit; to preach to perishing sinners till I drop down dead." It was as though God heard his prayer. His preaching on the streets drew huge crowds and his reputation for converting sinners spread. He became so effective that in 1857 he was invited to preach at the Moorfields Tabernacle in London, which had been George Whitefield's ministry home. Again, his messages were attended by great repentance and conversion, so much so that the elders of the church asked the now twenty-one-year-old college dropout if he would become their pastor.

It was a tempting offer. As successful a preacher as he was, there was little money in it. When he had received a £400 legacy from his uncle Arthur, he gave it to his aging mother. Still, he turned down the tabernacle offer and instead asked the elders to ordain him as an itinerant minister. He thus became a second-generation George Whitefield, and was often compared to the great eighteenth-century evangelist. As Henry departed London and then preached in France, Switzerland, Wales, and Scotland, the fruit was very much the same as Whitefield had produced a century before.

Finally, though, he returned to Dublin—and to great acclaim. As Michele Guinness has written, the local press took an interest because "Protestant preachers were weighted against each other like professional boxers." Henry was portrayed as a rival to Spurgeon, which was both silly and embarrassing, for all eminent preachers of the time were described in newspaper accounts with minute detail. Of Henry the *Liverpool Mercury* had written,

> A modest unassuming young man of twenty-one, of middle stature, wearing a frock coat that reaches to the knees and is buttoned almost up to the neckerchief. Long black hair, parted in the middle, and when the eyes are heaven-directed, reaching to the shoulders, forms the natural background and enclosure of the face, to which it lends

a classic or poetic grandeur, intensifying as it does every expression. His language is of the most childlike simplicity.

As Henry arrived in Ireland in February of 1858, he was met by a flurry of such press reports, including intrusive accounts of the death of his mother's first husband and of any misdeeds by any member of the Guinness clan. Still, the city was proud of its native son and prouder still that it was a Guinness who now drew international acclaim. Henry's first appearance on February 8 was described in full in Dublin's *Daily Express*.

> He appears to be not more than one and twenty years of age, his figure rather slight, and his features regular and complexion somewhat pale, which, combined with dark hair, worn long and thrown back from the forehead, tend to give him a striking and interesting appearance. In the pulpit his manner is quiet and unaffected, and characterized by an earnest simplicity which forcibly impresses itself on the listener. His gesture is remarkably graceful and appropriate, without the smallest approach to elocutionary display, and in addition to these, his voice is musical and well-modulated.

Within a week, newspaper accounts shifted from describing the young preacher's appearance to describing his effect on his audiences. Dublin had seen nothing like it in history. Souls were converted, churches began bulging, and the elite of the city turned out to see what this grandson of Arthur Guinness had to say for his God. Again, the *Daily Express*:

> He has now delivered nine discourses in this city since his arrival and the interest which he has excited, so far from abating, has daily increased, and will probably continue to do so during the present week . . . Few preachers have ever addressed congregations more select. They consisted of the elite of all denominations, including a considerable number of the Established Clergy. The wealth, the respectability, the cultivated intellect, as well as the evangelical piety of the city, have been represented in a measure unprecedented, we believe, on such an occasion in this country. Judges, members of Parliament, distinguished orators, Fellows of the College, the lights of the various professions, and, to a considerable extent, the rank and fashion of this gay metropolis, have been drawn out to a dissenting chapel which was thronged, even on weekdays, by this new attraction. On Wednesday morning the Lord Lieutenant was present, with the gentlemen of his Excellency's household; and yesterday morning we observed among the audience the Lord Chancellor, the Lord Justice of Appeal and Baron Pennefather.

It was as though Dublin could not hold him; he soon moved beyond the city into the rural areas where people were desperate to hear. As one observer wrote,

Without an exception the welcome he met with in the provinces resembled that in Dublin. Altogether nothing to compare with it had been known in Ireland within living memory. An announcement that he was to preach was enough to put the population on the move. The largest buildings available for his use failed to accommodate the numbers who thronged to hear him. A tidal-wave of popularity bore him along day after day. The local press everywhere chronicled and commented on his appearances as leading topics of interest.

Beyond his huge popularity and impact, we should note, too, his simplicity. There was no attempt to stir up emotions, no crafty plan to manipulate the crowd to a fever pitch. Instead, Henry Grattan Guinness simply preached the gospel—calmly, plainly, and with respect for his audiences. The *Daily Express* confirmed that there was no "cunning exhibition of oratorical fireworks, a dazzling stage effect, or theatrical contrivances to work up a 'galvanic revival.'" Instead, he was effective because "all his powers, intellectual and moral, are pervaded by a consecrating influence from on high."

The public and the press could not have missed the comparisons between Benjamin Lee, the head of the brewery, and the other Guinness who had become the John the Baptist of his age. In his thorough *Dark and Light: The Story of the Guinness Family*, Derek Wilson captures the contrasts that would have been obvious at the time.

They represented two elements—religious zeal and commercial flair—which had long jostled together in uncomfortable harness and which had now separated. Henry disdained money; Benjamin was well on his way to becoming a millionaire. The Dublin Guinness drew his wealth from beer; Henry was an advocate of temperance. The evangelist believed in the imminent return of Christ and the establishment of a new order; his cousin had made himself exceedingly comfortable in this world; Henry was the advocate of intense, personal faith; Benjamin represented a religious establishment which his Nonconformist relative could only regard as spiritually moribund.

Perhaps because of his tension with the Dublin Guinnesses or perhaps because of a sense of calling from God, Henry determined to make his way north to the industrial regions around Ulster and Belfast. Conditions in those cities were often as bad as Dublin's were becoming, and added to this was the turmoil of overheated political and religious tension. Henry Guinness was just the man to bring the message of Christ to souls in such a place. He had determined to rise above "party strife," to issue a call to Christ that transcended politics and petty religious division. The result was astonishing. Hardened men wept as he preached; it was not uncommon for some to fall as though dead under the press of conviction or "the Spirit's power." Though the preacher was ever calm and reasoned, the invisible force that accompanied his words broke both hearts and barriers to unity. One reporter wrote that when clergy of every denomination sat on the stage behind Guinness as he preached, "It was the first time that all these ministers had met on a platform broader than their churches."

The aftermath of the meetings was nearly as dramatic as the meetings themselves. Churches exploded with searching souls and ministers followed Henry's example in proclaiming a calm but unvarnished gospel of repentance and service to Christ. Between 1859 and 1862, Ulster's Protestant churches alone increased by a hundred thousand. When American evangelist Dwight Moody and soloist Ira Sankey preached throughout Ireland in 1874—largely at the invitation of John Grattan Guinness—it was obvious that they were harvesting where another man and another great work of God had gone before.

Henry was becoming one of the best-known preachers in the world. After his successes in the north of Ireland, he toured the United States. It was a pregnant moment for that troubled country, blessed as it was with a budding revival and cursed as it was by the specter of war over slavery and states' rights. Henry preached for ten weeks in Philadelphia and for seven in New York before visiting other towns throughout Canada and the western American states. When the tour finished he was exhausted. He had been preaching up to nine sermons a week for months on end and he needed a rest. He returned to England and vacationed in Ilfracombe in Devonshire. It would prove to be one of the most defining decisions of his life.

He was twenty-five at the time and had potential to become one of the most important Christian voices in his generation. But he was alone and increasingly felt the burden of it. At Ilfracombe, he met the woman who would bring this crisis to an end.

Her name was Fanny Fitzgerald and though she would become a source of joy to her husband, her past had been filled with tragedy. Her father was Major Edward Marlborough Fitzgerald, a member of one of Ireland's most celebrated aristocratic families. The major was the black sheep of that family, though, for he had decided to marry a Roman Catholic girl. It was a disastrous decision. His family abandoned him, his career was tarnished, and the marriage ended in divorce. Later, he married a fine woman named Mabel and that marriage was happy—but this is when the tragedies began.

Mabel died of tuberculosis, leaving her husband and five children behind. Fanny was the second of these. The major, now retired from the army, made a life as a successful journalist but always there were the financial pressures and the burdens of caring for each child. Then came the smallpox epidemic. Fanny's older brother, Gerald, succumbed to it and then Fanny fell ill as well. She would remember all her life how her father took her in his arms and told her that Gerald had died on the day the bells rang out for the wedding of Queen Victoria.

Henry Grattan Guinness and Fanny
(1861)

It was all too much for the man. He boarded a steamship destined for France, spent hours in the ship's saloon nursing a drink, wrote out a farewell letter, and then walked out onto the deck and jumped into the sea.

Shortly afterward, a London actuary and leading Quaker named Arthur West was just reading the newspaper account of Fitzgerald's death when his partner handed him a letter. West opened it and saw the signature of Edward Fitzgerald. In the letter, the obviously distraught man wrote of his concern for his four children, whose welfare he would "soon be unable to provide." The note ended with the line, "Before this reaches you, I shall be out of reach of any answer."

Fitzgerald had guessed correctly about the character of Arthur West, though. That evening, West went home to discuss the unfortunate children with his wife. The couple decided to adopt Fanny and to make sure the other children were placed in good homes. And so Fanny Fitzgerald found a life among Quakers and spent the next twenty years living with them, learning their ways, and serving the hurting of society at their side.

Her sufferings were not at an end, though. Her adoptive father had a reputation as a valiant soldier against slavery, but privately the strain was hard on his health; he suffered a stroke during Fanny's teen years. Unable to live with the burden he had become to his wife and stepdaughter, he took his own life. As Michele Guinness has written,

> By the time she was twenty-nine hard work and slender means had taken their toll. Whatever brilliant mental powers Fanny possessed were hidden behind her wan, sober appearance. Necessity, which had robbed her of her youth, had made her capable and competent, but never cold or hard. There was too much of the Irish in her for training to curb her fire and zest completely. When she opened her mouth to speak there was a sudden warmth and vivacity about her which commanded attention. The little tea parties of the Quaker and Brethren circles in which she moved tended to be dull, but one of the old ladies was overheard to say, "My dear, I do assure thee when Fanny Fitzgerald comes into the room she breaks the ice in a moment. Thou knows the way she has with her! Sets everyone talking, and puts the stiffest people at ease."

It was as she was seeking a rest herself—plans for a trip to Paris having fallen through—that she ended up in

Ilfracombe, where the famed Henry Grattan Guinness was recuperating from his American tour. She attended a service at which he preached, the two were introduced, and three months later they were married on October 2, 1860. Subsequently he would write, "I felt that I had found, for the first time in my life, a woman with a mind and soul that answer to my own. When with her I no longer felt alone."

It was good that Henry and Fanny shared an exceptional love, for the decades that followed their marriage were filled with turmoil and opposition. He would join the Plymouth Brethren and find that many of his former supporters felt this a step away from his nonpartisan approach to faith. He would also preach nonviolence just as the Civil War began in the United States, and this would make him a pariah, particularly among the British who were antislavery and who felt their cause was worth the fight. And he would champion an antialcohol conviction in an age when whiskey and beer flowed freely and when many in Ireland made their living producing one or the other.

Still, the Guinnesses preached on, traveling the world and mentoring young leaders when they could. They would influence some of the most fruitful Christians of their age. Among these was Dr. Thomas Barnardo. The Guinnesses had first met Barnardo when he was a Sunday school teacher in their Plymouth Brethren Church at Merrion Hall in Dublin. He was short, thin, bespectacled, and "almost monkey-like" in appearance and character. But he also wanted to make a difference for God and this endeared him to Henry, who befriended the boy and mentored him in the foundations of the Christian life. Barnardo came to believe that he should go to the mission field in China, but the counsel of friends prevailed and he ended up studying medicine at London Hospital. It was one of the most fortuitous decisions in the history of Christian benevolence.

While he tended his studies, he also involved himself in the evangelism and social outreach of a Plymouth Brethren church in London's East End. It was through this work that he was exposed to the horrors of Victorian slums. As Derek Wilson has powerfully written,

> He had been quite unprepared for the degree of squalor and human degradation which now confronted him—men taking refuge from misery in drink; women forced into prostitution to provide food for their families; people dying on the street of disease and starvation; children begging for coppers, their faces pinched with malnutrition, their health already broken by brutality or manual labor.

The tenderhearted doctor later recalled "rough-headed urchins, running with their feet bare through the puddles, and bonnetless girls, huddled in shawls, lolling against the door-posts." It was more than he could stand and though only a student at London Hospital he decided to lease an East End donkey stable and start a "ragged school" to get a few of these children off the street and to offer some minimal form of education. It was as he tended his waifs that he met Jim Jarvis.

This small boy is famous in the Barnardo story since it was through him that the good doctor came to understand the extent of the plagues that beset impoverished children in the Victorian age. In his book, *Night and Day*, Barnardo described his first meeting with the boy who would become his guide to the unseen plight of London's destitute children.

> One evening, the attendants at the Ragged School had met us as usual and at about half past nine o'clock were separating from their homes. A little lad, whome we had noticed listening very attentively during the evening, was amongst the last to leave, and his steps were slow and unwilling.
>
> "Come, my lad, had you better get home? It's very late. Mother will be coming for you."
>
> "Please sir, let me stop! Please let me stay. I won't do no harm."
>
> "Your mother will wonder what kept you so late."
>
> "I ain't got no mother."
>
> "Haven't got a mother, boy? Where do you live?"
>
> "Don't live nowhere."
>
> "Well, but where did you sleep last night?"
>
> "Down in Whitechapel, sir, along the Haymarket in one of them carts as is filled with hay; and I met a chap and he told me to come here to school, as perhaps you'd let me lie near the fire all night."

Little Jim Jarvis went on to explain to the wide-eyed doctor that many children slept on the streets of the city and he offered to show Barnardo what he meant. For the next weeks, night after night, the boy took the doctor on a tour of the hovels where London's orphaned children lived. They found children sleeping in barrels, on rooftops, under market stalls, and in any place that provided shelter from the wind and the rain and from the crooked adult who often kidnapped them for some evil purpose.

In the filthy, agonized faces of London's dispossessed children, Barnardo found his life's work. He began answering this call by taking his cause to the upper classes and using his inspiring gift for oratory to move the elite to action. He won support from Lord Shaftesbury, an evangelical, and from the famed banker, Robert Barclay. With their backing and influence among the wealthy, Barnardo was able to open a home for boys in Stepney in 1870. He would build many others, often buying pubs and music halls to convert them into children's homes. His work captured hearts throughout England, particularly after he began the practice of photographing each child when he first arrived, often gaunt and diseased, and then again months later when the child was happy and well. Barnardo sold postcards of these "before and after" photographs to raise money for his homes and to demonstrate the power of his work. The public responded with zeal and the work expanded dramatically in the following years.

By 1878, Barnardo had established fifty homes in

London alone. He had also begun a sort of town for homeless children which became a possibility when he and his wife, Syrie, were given a home in Barkingside, Essex, as a wedding gift. Barnardo turned this into a sixty-acre village for children, which remains the headquarters for the Barnardo foundation to this day. In 1906, the year after Barnardo died, there were thirteen hundred girls living there in sixty-six cottages.

He had also devised a plan for sending the destitute children of Britain to loving homes in the United States and Canada. This met with unprecedented success. Between 1882 and 1901, Barnardo's program sent 8,046 children to Canada, which meant that one-third of 1 percent of the entire Canadian population had come from Barnardo's homes overseas. By the time that he died in 1905, there were more than 8,000 children in his 132 homes, more than 4,000 more had been placed with families, and some 18,000 had been sent to happy homes in Canada and Australia.

That Thomas Barnardo accomplished such mighty works for God with the aid of Guinness mentoring, encouragement, and financial support is not well known. What is better known is the influence of the great China missionary, J. Hudson Taylor, upon their lives, for he would not only inflame their hearts for ministry in foreign lands but also become part of the Guinness story through marriage.

Hudson Taylor was converted at the age of seventeen while looking for a book to read in his father's library. He stumbled upon a tract titled "It Is Finished" and decided he had to know exactly what it was that was finished. By the time he had read the tract and searched out some of the answers for himself, he had, in his words, "made Christ his Savior." Months later, on December 2, 1849, he was spending time alone in prayer when the matter of China came to his mind. He was reminded of the time when at the age of four he had told his parents, "When I am a man I mean to be a missionary and go to China." This early episode and the sense he received in prayer as an adult together confirmed his call and he began to prepare to take the gospel to the Chinese people.

He spared himself nothing in the process. He immediately began sleeping on bare wood and eating very little. He moved into a noisy, poverty-ridden suburb and began to minister there, learning how to trust God for the money he needed to carry on. His body toughened, his faith deepened, and his vision for China became more keen. He came into contact with the Chinese Evangelization Society (CES), which made arrangements for him to train as a doctor at London Hospital in the East End. The gospel was exploding in influence in China, though, and when reports of these successes reached London the leaders of the CES and Taylor himself agreed that he should leave his studies immediately and begin the voyage to China.

His first years were troubled and without much success. He endured the ravages of a civil war, the opposition of anti-Western factions, the threat of cannibals and the callousness of other Western missionaries. Again, he learned the lessons of living by faith and of faithfully preaching when little seemed to come of it.

Home on furlough in 1865, he walked the beach at Brighton on June 25 and determined that he could not leave his field, that China was his life. He formed the China Inland Mission and began asking God for twenty-four missionaries to return with him. He also asked for money so that the mission could do its work unfettered. In hope, he opened a bank account with a paltry few pounds in it. He waited and he prayed. Miraculously, the famed Victorian preacher Charles Spurgeon heard Taylor speak and began championing his cause. Before long, he had £13,000 and the twenty-four missionaries he needed.

His years in China would be marked by the kind of opposition and despair most missionaries know. Children would die, assaults would wax and wane, and health would always be a challenge. Yet during fifty-one years in China, J. Hudson Taylor and his China Inland Mission would establish twenty mission stations, send nearly a thousand missionaries into the field, train some seven hundred Chinese workers, raise more than four million dollars,

From the Archives of OMF International; www.omf.org

Hudson Taylor

and leave behind a thriving Chinese church of 125,000. When modern readers watch the film *Chariots of Fire* and learn of Eric Liddell's missionary zeal for China, they should remember the work of J. Hudson Taylor. When modern readers turn on the evening news and learn that the Chinese Christian church today is the most rapidly growing center of Christianity in the world, they should remember J. Hudson Taylor. And when American Christians learn that some Chinese pastors have come to the United States to preach in "un-Christian Western lands," they should remember that it was J. Hudson Taylor who first embedded his own missionary zeal in the fledgling Chinese church.

Henry Guinness first met Taylor at a conference in Liverpool and was so impressed with his humility and

Hudson Taylor and family

intensity that he asked the missionary to address a gathering in his home. He must also have been struck by Taylor's appearance, for the missionary had taken to dressing like a Chinese coolie in order to pull down cultural barriers to the gospel he preached. It was not uncommon, then, to see Taylor in pigtail and silk short pants and shirt. This won him many a Chinese convert but also drew the resentment of many of his fellow countrymen. Such extremes in the service of God only endeared him to Henry Guinness, though, and the two became close friends.

In fact, internationally successful as Henry was, when he heard Taylor speak he immediately offered to join the work in China. This was at the same time that Thomas Barnardo was influenced by Taylor and yearned to give his life to Chinese missions. But Taylor was a wise man who knew every Christian had his own unique calling. He sensed that Barnardo was meant for other work and he told the Reverend Guinness that he could certainly do more good training young missionaries in England than going into the field himself.

This was a turning point in Henry and Fanny Guinness's lives. They already knew that most Christian denominations had schools for training ministers of their own but that no training was readily available for the kind of independent missionaries that Taylor and China Inland Mission needed. Still, they had not thought of themselves as meant to provide the answer to this challenge until Taylor changed their thinking. After much prayer and discussion, then, the

Guinnesses moved into a house in London's East End and began a one-house training school called Stepney Institute. It was located right in the heart of smoky factories and run-down tenements, in the kinds of neighborhoods where any serious missionary-in-training intent upon China must learn how to live. The students were required to preach in the open air and to give themselves to relief work as part of their training. It might not have seemed an inviting prospect for young men with other opportunities, but the school not only had a waiting list of students but eventually had to expand into new facilities. These facilities were at Harley House, Bow, and with the move the school then became known as the East London Institute for Home and Foreign Missions.

As with most great ventures in history, the times were perfectly prepared. Dwight Moody and Ira Sankey were making a second tour through England—during which they were hosted by the Guinnesses—and religious fervor was higher than it had been at any time since Wesley and Whitefield. Once again, as in the early days of Henry's ministry, thousands were converted, churches overflowed, and many offered their lives in Christian service. This meant a backlog of students for the Guinnesses' school, which came to be known as Harley House. In the spiritual zeal of the time, huge contributions flooded in. There was a ship, christened *Evangelist,* which was donated for ministry to crews on the docks. One wealthy man signed over his Derbyshire mansion and this became a school as well as

From the Archives of Michele Guinness

Fanny Guinness and children

a base for Barnardo's thriving work. And before long, land and buildings were donated for a Harley College, which became so successful it served as a model for Moody Bible College in the United States.

With men like Barnardo and Guinness living and ministering in the midst of its squalor, London's East End gained a reputation as a center of radical, nonconformist Christianity. This community of faith has been called an "Empire of Christian social concern in London's East End" and so vibrant was its flame that it lit still other torches around the world. Visitors to the Guinness home included Aimee Semple McPherson, Dwight Moody, General William Booth (founder of the Salvation Army), and even Lord Shaftesbury himself.

More important were the trained Christian workers dispatched to the unevangelized nations of the world. There were workers for China, of course, but also for Africa, since the adventures of David Livingstone and Henry Stanley along Lake Tanganyika—"Dr. Livingstone, I presume?"— had awakened Victorian missionary zeal. Indeed, as the twentieth century dawned, churches and mission stations in a hundred nations of the world bore testimony to the Guinness work at Harley House and College, much as the changed lives of thousands of orphans gave testament to the work of Barnardo, their friend.

As he neared the later years of his life, then, Henry Guinness was regarded as one of the great preachers of his age and as an innovator in Christian education. Yet as the new century drew near, many of his admirers came to know him best as a profound Christian author, one of the most important writers on Christian prophecy in his time. In this, too, he had profound impact, even on some of the most critical events of world history just about to unfold.

Though he had never finished college and once feared the loss of spiritual zeal if he gave himself to too much study, Henry had already begun to be a noted author when he likely deepened his commitment to Christian scholarship during a walk he took in 1886. His daughter, Lucy, later recounted the moment in her book, *For Such a Time*:

> Walking along the dreary street of a Yorkshire town, he paused to read a notice newly posted on the wall of a house. With his hands clasped behind his back, his high-crowned hat pushed to the back of his head, he read the poster with mounting indignation. It announced a series of lectures to be held in the neighborhood when a famous infidel would attack the character of Christ and the authority of the Bible.

The infidel was Charles Darwin, recent author of *On the Origin of the Species*. Though 50 percent of the population was illiterate and thus immune to the case Darwin would make, Henry feared that the rest of society, the thinkers and the upper classes, would take this man's ideas as true. He was appalled by the idea of an unplanned, unsustained creation used to imply atheistic conclusions. He altered his preaching schedule, read every book he could find that might answer Darwin's claims, and began teaching his students how to answer what he considered to be the most insidious lie of his age. Henry believed that while superstition and false religion might be the blinding force to the Christian gospel in China, it was pseudoscience that sought to win the day in England—and the church was largely unequipped to give an answer.

His reading in biblical history led him on to other topics, including biblical prophecy, which fascinated him. He became enthralled with the writing of the Swiss astronomer Jean-Philippe Loys de Chéseaux, who argued that if each day in the prophetic periods described by Daniel and in the book of Revelation were taken as a year, the resulting scheme fit perfectly with the astronomic cycles most astronomers knew to be true. Henry threw himself into further study in the field and reported his ideas to the world in his best-selling book *The Approaching End of the Age in Light of History, Prophecy and Science*. His work was so impressive—with its six-hundred-page appendix on astronomy—that it went through fourteen editions, earned

Henry the Doctor of Divinity, and resulted in his election to the Royal Astronomical Society.

In an already busy life, Henry Guinness would write more than twenty books, but perhaps none had a result equal to *Light for the Last Days*, published in 1886. As Frederic Mullally has explained, "He pinpointed 604 BC as a principal starting point of 'The Times of the Gentiles.' Measuring from that date, and from the starting point of the Mohammedan Calendar in AD 622, he calculated that 'the year 1917 is consequently doubly indicated as a final crisis date . . . clearly most critical in connection with Israel.'"

It was in 1917, of course, that British general Sir Edmund Allenby captured Jerusalem after four hundred years of Ottoman rule. Just months before this historic accomplishment, in June, Allenby was at the Grosvenor Hotel in London when he received a phone call from Sir Henry de Beauvoir de Lisle, a major-general in the British army, to congratulate him on his promotion to commander-in-chief. During the conversation, de Lisle made the point of saying, "Nothing can prevent you being in Jerusalem by 31 December." Allenby, surprised by the statement, asked, "How do you make that out?" It was then that de Lisle told the new commander of Dr. Henry Grattan Guinness's predictions in *Light for the Last Days*.

Jerusalem fell on December 9 of that year. Two days later, General Allenby entered Jerusalem, the first Christian commander to control the city in centuries. Though he was an excellent horseman, Allenby chose to dismount as he passed through the ancient city gates, in honor of Jesus Christ, whom Allenby believed was the only ruler with the right to ride into the city. Clearly, he had the predictions of Reverend Henry Guinness in mind as he did.

As astute as Henry Guinness's predictions about 1917 were, his writings about the restoration of the Jews were even more startling. Few living in his day would have expected that there might ever be a restoration of the Jews to their homeland in 1948. True, there were those who thought it the best policy for England (Lord Shaftesbury was one of the most vocal among these), but it was nearly inconceivable for most men at the time. Yet Henry Grattan Guinness, writing nearly sixty years before the event, predicted the miraculous event of 1948 when Israel again became a nation. This remains one of the most prescient works of an author in history.

It would have pleased Henry very much to know the role his writings played in the liberation of Jerusalem and then, later, in the restoration of the Jews to Israel, but if he heard of it at all it was in another life. He had died in 1910, one of the most revered men of his age.

His last decades had been as tumultuous as his early ones. His beloved Fanny, often in ill health, had suffered a stroke in 1892 that left her disabled until her death in 1898. Henry was still a vigorous man, then—trim, energetic, and lion-like with his great head of brilliant white hair. He clearly had no intentions of slowing down. He eventually married the twenty-six-year-old Grace Hurditch, daughter of a lifelong friend, and then set out with her on a five-year preaching tour around the world. Armed with letters of introduction, Henry preached in England and then visited the United States before ministering at length in Asia. In Australia, his first son with Grace, John Christopher, was born, and shortly after returning to England his second son, Paul Grattan, came into the world in 1908. Henry was already in his seventies at the time. Of his children with Fanny, three had died in infancy and one was still-born. Of those that survived—Harry, Geraldine, Lucy, and Whitfield—all were now in their thirties and forties and deeply committed to missionary work.

If a man can be measured by his children and his grand-children, then Henry Grattan Guinness did indeed lead a life of worth and honor. His oldest son, Harry, was a mission-ary/statesman who worked against cruel European exploi-tation in the Belgian Congo. His efforts led to audiences with King Leopold and President Theodore Roosevelt and changed that region of Africa forever. Henry's daughter, Lucy, proved to be a brilliant writer and eager adventurer. Though she died early of septicemia, she left two sons who extended her legacy. Henry, the older, was a Rockefeller Foundation research doctor and later a president of the Polio Foundation of America. Karl was an ordained American Episcopal priest who served as a chaplain in the U.S. armed forces.

Geraldine, Henry's older daughter, married J. Hudson

Taylor's son and spent her life working for China Inland Mission, influencing an entire generation of female missionaries. She was joined in her service in China by her brother, Dr. Whitfield Guinness. Geraldine would write the seminal biography of her father-in-law, *The Life of Hudson Taylor*, among other highly praised books, and she and her brother would serve the cause of their God in China in the face of persecution, war, disease, and death for decades to come.

The line of the faithful would continue. Among Henry Grattan Guinness's grandchildren would be Christian ministers and missionary medical doctors and Christian schoolmasters and Royal Air Force chaplains and missionaries to Asia, to name but a few of the careers in which these latter-day Guinnesses honored God. And the faith would live on in the great-grandchildren's time, as well, in champions of faith who reflect their great-grandfather's fire to this day.

But where, we should ask, did it all begin? How did it come to pass that one in ten of Arthur Guinness's children would give birth to a line of devoted Christians that would change the history of nations with their faith?

It is, unfortunately, impossible to say. But perhaps it came from something kindled in the first Arthur's heart. Perhaps as he listened to Wesley or worked to start Sunday schools in Ireland or fought for Catholic equality—perhaps during one of these moments something ignited in his soul. And perhaps, in a way we cannot know with certainty, that flame burned first in the heart of his soldier son and then came to full blaze in the life of his famed preacher grandson. Then, it is not hard to imagine, Guinnesses for a century after might well have lit their generational torches with the help of this flame. And so it continues through our time.

Again, we cannot know for sure. But we can know that this line of Guinnesses was the most distinct of all, as the tribute offered them by one historian makes clear.

Henry Grattan Guinness and Grace

As the 19th century drew to a close, the disparate branches of the Guinness family—brewers, bankers, and missionaries—were vigorously pursuing their varied interests in virtually every corner of the globe. A triple-stout Guinness beer, "West Indies Porter," had long since been lightening the white man's burden in the Caribbean and in a dozen other colonies of the far-flung British Empire. Banker Richard Seymour and his son Benjamin were in correspondence or personal contact with a network of overseas financial institutions, wherever an honest buck was to be made. But neither of these branches could match, in

Photo by Isaac Darnall

St. Stephen's Green, a private park, was relandscaped and gifted to the public by Arthur Edward Guinness in 1880.

adventurousness and energy, the deeds of the "Grattan" Guinnesses, spurred as they were not by materialistic ambition but by a deeply felt, inherited faith in what they believe to be the civilizing power of the Bible.

TWENTIETH-CENTURY GUINNESS

I t is difficult for our present, fast-paced age to understand how disorienting the speed of change must have
been for that nineteenth-century generation that was
forced to finish their lives in the twentieth century. Perhaps
the life of one man tells the tale.

Consider the life of Winston Churchill. He was born in
1874. Men still lived who had fought Napoleon. Ulysses S.
Grant was in his second term as the American president and
Karl Marx was just then in the British Library writing the

Communist Manifesto. Mark Twain had written none of the books for which he had become famous. Electricity, radio, television, and telephones were still unknown and only the year before Yale, Princeton, Columbia, and Rutgers universities had met to draw up the first rules for a new game. It was called "football."

When Churchill died ninety years later in 1965, men had orbited the earth, walked in space, and sent a probe to the surface of Venus. An automobile had already driven over six hundred miles per hour and sex-change operations had been successfully performed. Nuclear power had already come of age. Lyndon Johnson was the American president at that time and though he was considered an elderly man, he had been born when Churchill was already thirty-four. The year Churchill died, the Queen of England gave the Order of the British Empire to the Beatles. It was an honor Churchill had also received, yet for a far different contribution in a far different age.

How does one life absorb such change? What must it do to one's moorings, to that sense of connection to the flow of time and how a man experiences the rhythms of the world? Clearly, this was an ever-present challenge in Churchill's life and it frequently filled his thoughts: "I wonder often whether any other generation has seen such astounding revolutions of data and values as those through which we have lived. Scarcely anything material or established which I was brought up to believe was permanent and vital, has lasted. Everything I was sure or taught to be sure was impossible, has happened."

Churchill's words force us to ponder Guinness and what it must have been like for this thriving global firm to be suddenly caught up in the raging currents of change just as the twentieth century dawned. The Guinness family and the workers at the plant could have anticipated none of it, of course—not the wars or the technological leaps or the moral revolutions that would challenge everything they had known. Yet it seems that one of the great arts of living is to approach the onrushing future with such courage and flexibility that the power of change elevates, emboldens, and enlightens. Guinness modeled this art and it provides an example for our own age, when the pace of change more often seems poised to crush us than to lift us to greater heights.

As Guinness stepped into what appeared to be a promising new century, it had risen above all others to become the largest brewing company in the world. It employed more than 3,000 workers, with another 10,000 indirectly dependent on her production. The company's growth in the first years of the 1900s was beyond all expectation. In 1888, it had produced some 1.58 million barrels of beer; in 1899, this rose to 2.08 million. Yet in 1909, volume reached 2.77

million, and in 1914, just as the darks clouds of war were gathering in Europe, Guinness produced 3.54 million barrels. It was, simply put, the largest, the most productive, and the most prosperous producer of beer in human history.

Much of the company's success was due to the unique relationship of Guinness to the pubs that sold its product. Most of the pubs in Britain were brewery-owned establishments. These were called "tied" pubs, meaning they only sold the beer brewed by the firm that owned them. But Guinness was a "guest" beer, which meant that it could be sold both at the tied houses and at free pubs, which were unaffiliated with any brewery and could sell whatever beer the proprietor chose. Guinness, then, had access to the entire pub market without being burdened by owning and operating pubs itself. It was a gift of the regard in which it was held by the beer-drinking public, and the fruit of a wise choice to stay focused on what the company did best: brew beer.

As Guinness underwent this dramatic expansion, the board—chaired by Edward Cecil—became concerned about the quality of their exports and by how local agents were handling their product. In an age before rapid electronic communications, the best solution seemed to be to send men abroad to follow up on everything from shipping to sales throughout the world. Thus arose the season of the "Guinness World Traveller." Beginning in the early 1890s and continuing until World War I made such travel impossible, Guinness sent trusted men wherever its beer was sold to report back on any fact that might help the company improve on procedures and sales. Two men became legends in this role. J. C. Haines, a former brewer himself, became the World Traveller to Europe, the Middle East, and Australia. Arthur T. Shand traveled throughout the United States, Canada, Latin America, South Africa, and helped Haines with Australia.

It was an odd life. The two were away from home for months, even years at a time. They had to be meticulous, record-keeping men who were intensely loyal to the firm, while able to spend weeks at a time traveling alone. Their assignment was to record everything they could about how Guinness was shipped, how it was affected by climate, how it was sold at shops and pubs around the world, and what might be improved in bottling, labeling, marketing, and, of course, local brewing. The board also requested that the two men send home bottles of Guinness as they traveled so that they could see for themselves what agents abroad did to the Guinness product.

The journals and reports of Haines and Shand provide a window into both the turn-of-the-century beer trade and into the wider world at the time. There are detailed reports of "beer blowage," meaning the common experience of bottles exploding during shipping, and nearly poetic descriptions of Guinness casks strapped to loping camels and colorful accounts of turbaned Arabs drinking stout. What arise from nearly each page are the professionalism and great care these men poured into their work. Nothing was beyond their observation and reflection, as evidenced from this portion of Haines's report from Australia.

> No bursts and only the odd blower or two. The few breakages were due to too tight packing with insufficient straw. My experience has been that the straw envelopes are the best form of packing and the boxes should be made so that "spring" is allowed. When a box is packed so tight as to be nearly solid, a sudden jar on an end or corner invariably breaks a bottle or two. Once leakage sets in, the damp starts fermentation in the straw which generates heat and things go from bad to worse.

What we see from the writings of these men is an example of the kind of devotion to work and craft that was common at Guinness at the time. Men took pride in their skills and felt their area of responsibility nearly a sacred trust. They spoke of the minutest detail of a process related to brewing as though it was of utmost importance, as though each was a critical part of a vitally significant whole. It is inspiring to read of it. Haines and Shand were grand Victorian men who did not see their work as merely a source of income or something aside from the more important matters of life. Instead, they saw their work as an extension of their character, as a statement of what kind of men they were. A man's profession was where he demonstrated to the world who he was, and why he deserved the things his labors allowed him to possess. It was a far different age from ours and with far different values regarding work, but it is refreshing to read the words of these men, sometimes half a world from home, tending the smallest matter of a label or the design of a bottle or the angle of a sign out of devotion to their bosses in Dublin and, perhaps as important, out of a healthy regard for themselves and their trusted place in the world.

The reach of Guinness during this period was nearly absurd. When an Antarctic expedition in 1933 returned to the site of an earlier expedition in 1929, a member of the team reported that at the abandoned station "there were also four bottles of Guinness on a shelf, which, although frozen, were put to excellent use." Ralph Patteson Cobbold, the famed British explorer, even found Guinness on sale in the Hindu Kush range of the Pamir Mountains in Central Asia. In his *Innermost Asia: Travel and Sports in the Pamirs*, Cobbold wrote, "I directed my attention to a wine and spirit store where I spied, gently to my delight, the magic harp of Guinness inscribed on imperial pints of stout. The price was stiff—eight shillings a bottle—but it didn't seem exorbitant when one considered the distance it had traveled from its native land. The stout was excellent."

Feeling the optimism of the age and of its own success, Guinness began to prepare for even greater growth. The board funded continuous expansion at St. James's Gate and also decided to purchase a fleet of steamships for conveying its product to strategic ports. In 1913, the *W. M. Barkley* was built and the *Carrowdore* was purchased. A year later, in 1914, the *Clareisland* and *Clarecastle* were begun with hopes that they could be launched in 1915. At about the same time, Edward Cecil purchased a hundred-acre plot along the Manchester Ship Canal, where he intended to build a second brewery of massive proportions. His plan, as he explained it to the board, was to build a plant so huge that it would be able to produce four times as much brew as the St. James's Gate plant had in 1912. It was a grand scheme, fit for the promise of the new century and bolstered by the record-breaking pace of Guinness's explosive growth.

Yet, as with so many plans and hopes at the time, few of these aims were achieved. War cruelly intervened, with a ferocity that none could ever have imagined. In the fall of 1914, what poets later called the "guns of August" began to spew death, and before they were silenced four years later, more than ten million men had died and more than twice that number had been wounded. It would mean the loss of a generation of European manhood and an equally tragic loss of tradition, hope, and faith for decades after. When it was done, it had solved little but it had confirmed the follies of a dying age to those who came to be known as "the lost generation."

Crisis once again forced the Guinness corporate values to the surface. In an astonishingly gracious move, the firm promised to hold the job of any man who enlisted in the armed forces and to pay him half his salary while he served. This kept wives and children at home from suffering financially and allowed men in uniform to focus on their fight rather than suffer distraction from fear for their families' well-being.

Some one hundred men volunteered immediately as part of the St. James's Gate Division of the St. John Ambulance Brigade and more than five hundred enlisted soon afterward. This meant that the brewery lost nearly 20 percent of its workforce, and it anticipated still other declines to come. Though the firm had been experiencing unprecedented growth in the years leading up to the war, sales dropped 10 percent for the first two years of the conflict. By 1917, though, sales were half what they had been before the war. Challenges in production plagued the firm. Raw materials were scarce and the price of barley skyrocketed because war needs converted barley fields to wheat fields instead. It was a horrible time, both because of the war and because of the firm's decline at home; board members feared that the challenges might set the company back twenty years.

Still the Guinness spirit prevailed and nothing showed this as much as the story of survivors of a tragedy during the war. In 1917, the *W. M. Barkley*, the first Guinness steamship that had since been converted to military use, was torpedoed by a German U-boat off Kish Lightship. The boat sank and most of the crew were lost, but the survivors told a tale that lived on in Guinness lore. As crewman Thomas McGlue recalled,

> We rowed away from the *Barkley* so as not to get dragged under. Then we saw the U-boat lying astern. I thought

she was a collier, she looked so big. There were seven Germans in the conning tower, all looking down at us through binoculars. We hailed the captain and asked him to pick us up. He called us alongside and then he asked us the name of our boat, the cargo she was carrying, who the owners were and where she was registered, and where she was bound to. He spoke better English than we did. . . . He said we could go . . . Then he pointed out the shore lights and told us to steer for them. The submarine slipped away and we were left alone, with hogsheads of stout bobbing all around us. The *Barkley* had broken and gone down very quietly.

We tried to row for the Kish, but it might have been America for all the way we made. We put out the sea anchor and sat there shouting all night . . . At last, we saw a black shape coming up. She was the *Donnet Head*, a collier bound for Dublin. She took us aboard and tied the lifeboat alongside. We got into Dublin at 5 a.m. and an official put us in the Custom House at the point of the Wall, where there was a big fire. That was welcome, because we were wet through and I'd spend the night in my shirtsleeves. But we weren't very pleased to be kept there three hours. Then a man came in and asked "Are you aliens?" I said, "Yes, we're aliens from Dublin." He seemed to lose interest then, so we walked out and got back in the lifeboat and rowed it up to Custom House Quay. The Guinness superintendent produced a bottle of brandy and some dry clothes.

It was a tale that Guinness men passed from generation to generation and it buoyed spirits during the dark years of the war. And spirits needed strengthening, for the blows to Guinness did not seem to end. Some of these blows came from the government in London. During the war, the British parliament decided to raise taxes on beer and foolishly mandated a reduction in the gravity of beer, meaning that the alcohol content was lower. This only made the beer less attractive to consumers and more likely to spoil. Then, in another folly, Parliament required pubs to close at eleven p.m., which reduced Guinness sales even further. All of this combined to make the war years among the most disastrous of all for the Guinness firm.

When the war was ended, British losses amounted to more than 700,000 with more than 1.6 million wounded returning home in search of jobs and some sense of normality. It was a difficult promise to fulfill, particularly given the events unfolding in Ireland.

Guinness's homeland was just then in the birth pangs of independence. There had been home rule (self-government) advocates in Ireland for generations. This had stirred tensions throughout the land, where disagreements persisted as to whether Ireland should accept a measure of independence within the United Kingdom or whether she should hold out for complete autonomy. Cooler heads wanted home rule. More radical groups like Sinn Féin wanted nothing less than a nation equal to and separate from England. The British parliament finally passed a Third

Home Rule Act, which included a plan for the partition of Ireland into a Protestant piece of Ulster in the north, and a Dublin-based, more Roman Catholic league of counties in the south. The implementation of the plan was interrupted by the onset of World War I, though, and all action was postponed.

Still, the dream of Irish independence lived. In 1916, a relatively small group of revolutionaries incited what came to be known as the Easter Rising. It lasted less than a week and never grew beyond Dublin, because it didn't have nationwide support. But the British decision to callously execute the leaders of the insurrection achieved what the rising itself had not: it stirred popular animosity against the British government throughout Ireland. Violent years followed, with bombings and assassinations and misery throughout the land. Finally, in 1919, Ireland declared her independence, which led to still more bloodshed with England. It was not until 1922 that British and Irish negotiators agreed to a self-governing Irish Free State—a dominion within the British Empire equal to Australia or Canada. Six of Ireland's thirty-two counties formed them-selves into a separate Northern Ireland and remained part of the United Kingdom. It would not be until two and a half decades later, in 1949, that the lower twenty-six coun-ties formed the Republic of Ireland and left the British Commonwealth completely.

These upheavals plagued Guinness—the company and the family—much as it did the whole of the Irish people.

Guinness family members split over the political issues and argued heatedly at family dinners—and even on the floor of Parliament. Workers broke out into fistfights on the brewery floor and arguments robbed the peace of mealtimes and the fellowship of a pint after work. More threatening still were the sounds of explosions and the great billows of smoke that reached to the brewery and made men look up from their labors in fear.

Still, even in these times, the Guinness men were agents of good. The revered Dr. Lumsden was a cherished figure in these years, darting among the wounded during a battle or training first aid workers in makeshift classes at the Guinness plant. Guinness family members, even while disagreeing among themselves, urged moderation and humanity among all factions and modeled a devotion to Ireland that rose above party strife. They also remained an image of refinement and style that made many believe a better day might return. During the worst of some of the conflicts, the chairman of the Guinness board routinely gave brewery staff short trips on his magnificent boat, the *Fantome*. A guest on one of these trips recalled a Sunday morning sail down the Liffey: "he sat in a deck chair, being offered drinks . . . when shouting broke out between the buildings on the bank and he could see men firing at each other with great danger to life and limb, which did not affect the life on board though there was a separation of no more than 400 yards."

It was easy to feel aloof from the street battles on an

expensive sailboat, but Guinness was unable to float above the inevitable economic disruptions of the postwar years. The company had experienced dramatic growth prior to the war and then had dropped production by nearly half during the dark days from 1914 to 1918. A recovery seemed near in 1920, when Guinness sales returned to prewar levels and then rose 10 percent in 1921. In 1922, though, sales began falling, and they would not recover for quite some time. This was due to a number of factors. The lower gravity mandated by the government during the war made the beer less desirable. In addition, the Irish government maintained a tax on beer that was equal to that imposed by the United Kingdom during the war. To all of this was added the complete loss of the Guinness market in the United States because of the advent of Prohibition. We should take time to understand this moment in U.S. history, not only to better comprehend Guinness's challenges at the time but also to grasp attitudes toward beer and alcohol that exist in America to this day.

There had long been efforts for prohibition of alcohol sales in the United States and it is not hard to understand why. From the earliest days of the colonial era, alcohol had played a vast role in nearly every part of life. Men paid for goods with whiskey, doctors treated wounds with wine, and political events were awash with strong drink cynically provided by the politicians themselves. Inebriated men made easy political targets. Whiskey was so prized that when the new federal government decided to tax alcohol sales in 1791, a revolt ensued known to history as the Whiskey Rebellion.

The popular attitude toward drink was that of earlier generations of Christians: alcohol in moderation is a grace of life but drunkenness is both sin and a plague upon society. As pioneers moved westward and small towns began to dot the plains, the negative effects of alcohol became more pronounced. It would take only a few hard drinking men to terrorize a small community, and only one drunken father and husband to leave a family destitute on the dangerous frontier. Naturally, antidrink societies formed—understandably led by women—and many a tension arose between the "dry" and "wet" factions of the American west.

As antialcohol sentiments increased, entire states banned alcohol sales. Maine was first in 1851, with Rhode Island, Massachusetts, and Vermont following in 1852. A year later, Michigan followed suit, as did Connecticut in 1854. These laws were loosely and incompetently enforced, though, and this only led to increased frustration on the part of temperance groups. Finally, antialcohol sentiments merged with religious beliefs and led to the formation of the Woman's Christian Temperance Union in 1874. This body thrived in the rural sections of the country and led, in time, to the rise of the legendary Carrie Nation—the woman who, in reaction to her first husband's alcoholism, took axe in hand and destroyed saloons all over the Midwest. Her exploits captured the imagination of many

Americans and, in an age of anticorruption reform, the war on alcohol gathered strength.

In retrospect, brewers seemed unaware of these currents of change. Believing rightly that beer and alcohol had always been a valued part of American life, brewers throughout the United States saw little threat in the gathering antialcohol storm. They continued to cite the American heritage of moderate alcohol use and even proclaimed a favorite truism from the era of the founding fathers: "The brewery is the best pharmacy." They were tragically unaware of their times. They were unable to see what would come of women gaining political power, many of these women armed with tales of the devastation excessive drink had meant for their families. They could not have understood how World War I would lead to fiery anti-German sentiment and how this in turn would focus rage on the largely German trade of brewing beer. And they could not have foreseen how many a politician, riding an anticorruption wave, would blame alcohol for most of the country's woes and thus come to proclaim prohibition of alcohol as a national panacea. When brewers in America did wake up to the prevailing trends, there was little they could do.

The legislation that would lead to the Prohibition began in 1917 with the passage of the Food Control Act, which gave Woodrow Wilson the authority to regulate the manufacture of beer and wine. Prohibitionists had worked behind the scenes for the passage of the bill, knowing that it was a first step toward outlawing alcohol sales, and

Wilson complied. He required a reduction in beer sales of 30 percent and dramatically limited the amount of alcohol a beer could contain. It was only a beginning. Immediately, a constitutional amendment was proposed for prohibiting intoxicating drink entirely. This amendment passed in January of 1919 but it needed accompanying legislation to assure enforcement. In the famous Volstead Act that ensued, an intoxicating beverage was defined as anything containing more than 5 percent alcohol. Oddly, President Wilson vetoed the act, Congress overrode, and the Supreme Court upheld the act when brewers filed a desperate suit to bring the prohibition mania to an end. On January 17, 1920, the United States became a dry nation.

It would prove to be one of the most foolish governmental acts in American history, a point of discussion on morality and law for generations to come. It had little popular support. A poll taken in 1926 revealed that only 19 percent of Americans favored Prohibition and the Eighteenth Amendment that made it law. Prohibition was thus a blow to democracy. It was also a blow to law and order. The more than 177,000 saloons in America prior to Prohibition merely went private, so that in New York alone some 32,000 speakeasies thrived, many eventually providing still other illegal activities, such as prostitution, among their benefits of membership. These establishments were often serviced by thousands of smugglers who focused their efforts on whiskey, gin, and rum. Prohibition, then, not only led to illegal trade in alcohol, but it also meant that increasing numbers of Americans were drinking hard liquor rather than the more moderate and healthy beer. In short, Prohibition increased the consumption of hard liquor in America.

It also increased home-brewing. As H. L. Mencken wrote at the time, "Every second household has become a home-brewer . . . In one American city of 750,000 inhabitants there are now 100 shops devoted exclusively to the sale of beer-making supplies, and lately the proprietor of one of them, by no means the largest, told me that he sold 2,000 pounds of malt-syrup a day."

The miseries, mysteries, and manipulations of Prohibition would last nearly a decade before the Roman Catholic presidential candidate, Al Smith of New York, made repeal a major theme of his campaign. Though Smith lost his race for the White House, he made repeal acceptable and soon such luminaries as General "Black Jack" Pershing, Walter Chrysler, Harvey Firestone, and John Rockefeller were echoing Smith's cry for change.

Rockefeller was perhaps the most interesting of these because he did not drink alcohol—but he did recognize the failure of Prohibition.

Failure of the Eighteenth Amendment has demonstrated that the majority of this country are not yet ready for total abstinence, at least when it is attempted through legal coercion. The next best thing—many people think it a better thing—is temperance. Therefore, as I sought to support total abstinence when its achievement seemed possible, so now, and with equal vigor, I would support temperance.

It fell to the newly elected Franklin Delano Roosevelt to call for an end to the madness. Barely a week after taking office, Roosevelt asked Congress to raise the legal alcohol limit of beer to 3.2 percent. Congress complied, and though the official end of Prohibition would await the passage of the Twenty-first Amendment in 1933, the end of this misguided policy had come.

Prohibition stands as a testimony to the damage that can be done through ignorance of the benefits of beer. Rather than emphasize beer as an antidote to drunkenness, as a healthy alternative to harder drinks that, in excess, ruined men's lives, Prohibitionists treated all alcohol as the same. This not only meant that consumption of hard liquor rose during Prohibition, but that the idling of breweries removed the societal benefits of beer in the post-Prohibition years. Prior to Prohibition there had been sixteen hundred breweries in America. Only seven hundred reopened when Prohibition was repealed, but more than five hundred of those soon failed, burdened as they were with out-of-date equipment and inadequate financing. This meant, again, during the critical 1930s when beer might have served a Depression-era people well, hard liquor ruled the day. Lives were destroyed; crime and poverty spread as a result. Prohibition had served no better purpose than to ban moderation, both during its reign and in the difficult years afterward.

For Guinness, Prohibition meant a complete loss of the American market at a time when brewing was taxed and troubled in Ireland and domestic brands were making inroads in places like Australia and South Africa. Still, the Guinness spirit prevailed. With the brewery running at low capacity because of the loss in sales, a brilliant young scientist named Alan McMullen took advantage of the lag to test his new ideas. McMullen was head of the Guinness research department and he was convinced that a more scientific approach to brewing could yield good results. All he needed was access to some usually tightly scheduled equipment to prove his ideas. Gaining permission to take over a portion of the brewery, McMullen developed a process for continuous sterilization and did studies on the nitrogen content in barley, both of which allowed Guinness to improve its product and increase sales.

McMullen's scientific approach brought such good results that it infected the Guinness culture. Now, more careful tracking of sales, tighter monitoring of pricing, and an even more studied approach to shipping ensued. Of all the Guinness board members at the time, the man who best understood the demands of the age, the Guinness culture, and modern methods of business was Ben Newbold. In a manner that may have been influenced by the ways of Dr. John Lumsden, Newbold decided in 1926 to travel throughout England to gain firsthand information about the distribution of beer. For two months he interviewed bottlers, retailers, and, more important, consumers in order to understand what was working, what wasn't, and how Guinness could improve market share. His conclusions were as far-reaching as Lumsden's had been. His most important recommendations had to do with marketing.

> Apart from the "selling" organization of our customers (the bottlers) we have relied on our stout selling itself. It is obviously financially impossible for us for many years to come to get Guinness back to the position of selling itself (as it did in prewar days) by being apart from its "character" the best value for money to the consumer. Until it sells itself again it would seem that we must take steps to sell it ourselves, either by offering extra inducements to those handling it, or by creating a public demand by gravity or price, or by advertising, or by a much stronger selling organization of our own, or perhaps by a little of all of them.

This matter of advertising had been a touchy subject at Guinness. In 1909, Edward Cecil had said, "It is our general rule to advertise in no way. We never do so in England or Ireland." It was a luxury of Guinness at the time, when sales were soaring and the reputation of the product sold itself. Now, though, in the postwar 1920s, the situation was different. Newbold worked hard to convince the board times had changed and that the company should move quickly toward an advertising plan, noting that "it is easier for us (and much less expensive) to retain ground we have captured than to regain ground when it has been lost." As Guinness archivist Eibhlin Roche recounted to author Bill Yenne, "Lord Iveagh [Edward Cecil] felt that if you needed to advertise a product this meant that you had an inferior product, but Ben Newbold eventually convinced him that Guinness should advertise. Newbold was the first Guinness marketer. I'd definitely consider him as one of the greats."

This shift came at the end of Edward Cecil's life. He approved the first Guinness steps toward advertising at a board meeting on August 30, 1927. Just weeks later, on October 27, he died. He was eighty years old and had led the company since 1876—through astonishing growth, the transition to a publicly owned company, the expansion before and then the drastic decline after the Great War, and, at the very end of his life, the challenges of business in a new and roiling century. He had given his life to the brewery and it had given him unprecedented wealth: his estate was valued at £13.5 million when he died, the most of any estate to that time in British history. He was part of a rare breed: a Victorian gentleman who had carried his firm successfully into the next century. Though his company was troubled and in desperate need of new methods, it could hope to prosper in the decades to come because Edward Cecil Guinness had so long been at the helm.

The chairmanship of the Guinness board fell to Edward Cecil's eldest son, Rupert. Though it was his father's wish, it could not have been an easy choice. Rupert was fifty-three years old at the time and had almost no previous experience at the brewery. Moreover, he was viewed by many in the family as an odd man, a loner given more to staring at microorganisms through a microscope than to people, more to travel and dreaming than to beer. It was a perception that plagued him as he took the helm of the brewery.

In his childhood he had shared a nanny with Winston Churchill and the two had played by the hour, as boys will often do. On one occasion of rowdiness, young Winston lashed Rupert across the eye with a whip. The clumsy treatment of the wound by a doctor left permanent scarring. Years later, when both men were in their eighties, Churchill turned to the then second Lord Iveagh and said, "I say, Rupert, do you remember that fight we had in Dublin?" Both men cherished the memory of those more innocent days.

Rupert would grow into manhood bathed in the disapproving glare of his family. He did not perform well in school and this was unacceptable for a Guinness. He was thought stupid and lazy. He was tested for everything from eye trouble to mental disturbance but no cause for his failures came to light. The truth was that he suffered from dyslexia, but this was an unknown condition in his day and so he endured unending chastisement and ridicule. His parents might have known better. When seven-year-old Rupert got his hands on his father's new microscope, he became fascinated with the other universe he found, which began a lifelong passion for scientific investigation. It was not the mark of a slow or uninterested boy. It was instead the sign of a boy who could teach himself better than he could be taught in school, but it would not be until adulthood that his gifts were recognized and prized.

At Eton and later at Cambridge he was a poor student but a beloved friend. Even his headmaster at Eton wrote that Rupert was "a model of good conduct and good temper to all . . . I think that his character is one of the most perfect I have ever met with in a boy here and I can hardly think it possible that he could ever do anything discreditable." Then, the headmaster added, "I wish his ability approached his character in excellence."

He excelled not only at his scientific pursuits but at rowing. At Cambridge he defeated the champion in Diamond Sculls and became a campus hero. In time, he emerged as the undisputed amateur sculling champion of England and this brought him a kind of social success he had never known before. His athletic career ended, though, when he was diagnosed with a weak heart and forbidden to compete. He turned, again, to his microscope and his quiet hours and looked on as his disappointed father lavished attention on Rupert's younger brothers, Ernest and Walter.

He served in the Boer War at the end of the twentieth century as chief of staff to Sir William Thomson and distinguished himself, though he became ill with severe dysentery and enteric fever. He returned home, was decorated for service to his country, and began working as his father's secretary. He married Lady Gwendolin Onslow sometime after and Edward Cecil blessed the new couple with the generous wedding gift of £5 million.

He might have passed his days as the wealthy young men of his time usually did: at his club and at sport. Rupert was made of better stuff, though, and this seems to have come as a surprise to nearly everyone who knew him. He had absorbed the Guinness concern for the needy, that family sense of obligation to use wealth for the good of mankind. When he received the wedding gift from his father, he did not set himself up in fashion. Instead, he moved his new bride into a home in the slums and launched a crusade to ease the plight of the poor. His social class was scandalized. The common man in Ireland was moved. And the media barely knew what to make of it. As one newspaper reported, "It speaks well for disinterested public service in this country that a man whose recreations are yachting, rowing, shooting and golf, and whose clubs are the Beefsteak, Leander, Carlton, Garrick and Royal Yacht Squadron should be ready to work for the weak and the needy."

It was not a gimmick or a short-lived scheme. Rupert and Gwendolin lived in the slums of Shoreditch for seven years. And they knew tragedy. In 1906, a pregnant Gwendolin was involved in a bad car accident and the baby boy she was carrying at the time was born prematurely. He lived only thirty-six hours. In the manner of his forebears, Rupert let tragedy move him to more meaningful service. He served on the London City Council and became a champion of humanitarian reforms, particularly of those reforms pertaining to children. He gained a reputation as a compassionate soul and a fierce fighter. He was elected to Parliament representing Haggerston in 1908 and in 1912 he was elected for Southend-on-Sea. He served in that seat for more than two and a half decades, until 1927, when his father's death placed him in charge of the Guinness brewery, elevated him to his father's peerage, and granted him a seat in the House of Lords. His wife, Gwendolin, decided to continue their fight for the impoverished on her own. She stood for her husband's seat in Parliament and won, becoming one of the early female members of Parliament in British history. The United Kingdom now had both a member of the House of Lords and a female MP who had lived in slums, championed the cause of the poor, and intended to do so until they died. It was part of the Guinness way.

The brewery Rupert oversaw as of 1927 was a far different place than the one his great ancestor had purchased. From the original four acres leased in 1759, the plant had now grown to more than sixty acres. The brewery included so many buildings spread over such a large space that it required eight miles of train track to connect them all effectively. There were fermenting rooms and vat houses and stables and cooperage shops and cask-washing sheds and train barns and massive storerooms for hop and malt. There were docks and ships and every kind of garage and maintenance building imaginable. Scurrying amongst them all were trucks and rail cars and horse-drawn wagons. The

Guinness output was so profuse that the labels it printed in 1930 alone—Guinness did not bottle its own beer but it did print all its own labels—would have nearly stretched around the earth.

Rupert would become chairman of the Guinness board shortly before the worse economic crisis to befall the Western world. On October 29, 1929, the New York Stock Exchange collapsed, a day that would live in history as Black Tuesday. The British brewing industry declined by more than 20 percent over the next years, but this was little compared to the devastation that wracked the Irish economy. Guinness sales fell to half the company's 1927 levels by 1932—although wise leadership and some fortunate occurrences would allow the company to double its 1914 revenue by 1939. This came about, in part, because the United States ended Prohibition in 1933, restoring the American market, and because Guinness board member Ben Newbold won his case for advertising.

After Edward Cecil finally lifted the advertising ban in 1927, Guinness hired the advertising firm of S. H. Benson and began testing marketing campaigns. More than likely, some board members had yet to be convinced. The Benson firm encouraged Guinness to take a test run in Glasgow, where Guinness sales had been in decline since 1914 despite the presence of a sizeable Irish population. The campaign began in the fall of 1927, and by April 1928, sales were up by 7.3 percent. For those who needed further proof, when advertising was employed in England—

where Guinness sales had shrunk by some 6.8 percent—sales also rose dramatically.

Guinness became committed to advertising and the partnership with Benson would produce some of the most famous slogans and campaigns in advertising history. Early on, Benson suggested the slogan, "Guinness is Good for You." This came from marketing research that showed people actually "felt good" after drinking a Guinness. The slogan stuck and was used for decades to come. It was the perfect sentiment at the perfect time and it anticipated the later research that alcohol in moderation was both healthy and invigorating.

Creating this slogan was the first step, but when S. H. Benson paired Guinness with John Gilroy, one if its illustrators, the Guinness campaigns began capturing global attention. Gilroy was a balding, bespectacled man who understood the whimsy needed to win a weary public to the Guinness brand. He was an Englishman who had attended Durham University before World War I interrupted his studies. He'd served in the Royal Field Artillery until war's end and then resumed his studies at the Royal College of Art in London. After graduation, Gilroy went to work for the Benson firm. He was a gifted artist who would later paint portraits of Winston Churchill, Sir John Gielgud, Edward Heath, Pope John XXIII, and many members of the royal family. Queen Elizabeth II would sit for a Gilroy portrait when the artist was eighty-two.

He joined Benson in 1925 and not long after worked on

the first Guinness campaign, which centered on the slogan, "Guinness for Strength." This included famous images of a man—the same man who was featured in much of Gilroy's Guinness art and was actually a self-portrait—carrying a girder. By 1935, Gilroy was producing advertisements involving myriad animals, which some began to call the "Guinness Zoo." It was a novel approach. "I have always been a jolly man," Gilroy later said, "and I thought the Guinness campaign needed a touch of humor." While attending the Bertram Mills Circus one day, Gilroy had the idea for a menagerie of animals that would, over time, balance Guinness on their snouts or steal Guinness from zookeepers or, during the war, even fly in formation delivering Guinness.

The advertisements met with joyous popular appeal. The intense interest the public gave to each new ad was confirmed in 1936 when a popular Guinness poster showed an ostrich swallowing a zookeeper's pint glass of Guinness. The pint in the ostrich's long neck was right side up, though, and letters flooded the Benson and Guinness offices. Thousands of Guinness drinkers were apparently concerned that this fictional ostrich could not drink his Guinness if the pint glass stuck in his long neck was not turned downward. When the same ad was reissued in 1952, it was accompanied by a poem that read:

The ostrich, travelers recall,
Enjoys his Guinness, glass and all

How sad the Guinness takes so long
To get where it makes him strong!

Over the following years, Gilroy would fashion campaigns around slogans like "It's a Lovely Day for a Guinness," "Guinness as Usual," and "My Goodness! My Guinness!" Always there was the cartoon self-portrait of Gilroy, running frantically after a beer-stealing seal or marveling at a toucan balancing two pints of brew on his beak. This toucan was perhaps the most famous of Gilroy's Guinness symbols and was often accompanied by verse.

If he can say as you can
Guinness is good for you.
How grand to be a Toucan
Just think what Toucan do.

Or,

Toucans in the nests agree
Guinness is good for you.
Open some today and see
What one or Toucan do.

Gilroy's work for Guinness would become legendary and would extend well into the 1960s, leaving a legacy of more than a hundred posters over thirty-five years. His skill was such that Walt Disney offered him a lucrative job in Hollywood. Gilroy turned him down. David Ogilvy, the father of British advertising, has said that Gilroy's posters "made Guinness part of the warp and woof of English life and have never been excelled—anywhere."

The strength of Guinness's advertising is revealed, in part, by some of the luminaries who were inspired by it. James Joyce, among Ireland's greatest writers, not only mentioned Guinness dozens of times in his works, but once suggested his own idea for a Guinness slogan: "The free, the flow, the frothy freshener." (Clearly, Guinness was less than impressed, because it stayed with "Guinness Is Good for You.") Dorothy Sayers, who became famous for her Lord Peter Wimsey mystery stories, worked for Benson from 1922 to 1931 and partnered with Gilroy on a number of his campaigns. The first toucan jingle mentioned above is hers.

Throughout the 1930s, Guinness increased its sales largely on the strength of its advertising. This inspired the board to begin preparing for further expansion. In 1936, the company opened a new brewery about twenty-five miles north of central London at Park Royal. The plant became essential to Guinness's future success, producing nearly a third of the total company output by 1939. Shortly after World War II, the plant exceeded the production at St. James's Gate.

During this time, Guinness also acquired a brewery in the United States. In 1934, the E. J. Burke firm, a Guinness distributor, opened Burke Brewery Inc. in New York within view of the Manhattan skyline. This venture was not the success that Park Royal was, though. The brewery opened during the darkest days of the Great Depression, amidst powerful competition and with national brand recognition still recovering from the complete market shutdown of Prohibition. To keep the firm from bankruptcy and to exploit the opportunity of an existing brewery in the exploding United States market, Guinness bought the facility in 1943, though production of stout had to await the end of World War II.

Yet it was World War II that confirmed just how essential to life Guinness had become for many a man in the United Kingdom. When Hitler's army invaded Poland on September 1, 1939, England and France declared war against Germany. Millions of men marched into battle and Guinness determined to provide what support it could. It was helped by a shift in attitude toward beer on the part of the British government. During World War I, many officials had viewed beer as a hindrance to both soldiers and civilian laborers alike. By World War II, though—thanks in large part to Guinness advertising and the new plant at Park Royal, both of which made Guinness as much English as it was Irish—the government understood the value of Guinness in connecting men to their homeland and in buoying their spirits at war. Guinness was provided free of charge to hospitals, shipped to men at the front, and served at a discount to all men in uniform at home. The official attitude toward beer was so transformed that the British Army asked Guinness to set aside 5 percent of its production for the troops.

Guinness was happy to comply and in December of 1939, in the lull before the expected invasion of France, each man at the front was given a bottle of Guinness with his Christmas dinner. It had not been an easy request to fulfill. With so many Guinness staff at war, the plant required hundreds of additional workers to make sure each soldier got his bottle of brew by December 25. Patriots arose. Volunteers lined up outside the brewery gates, some of them retired Guinness employees and some veterans of World War I. The Red Cross sent workers, and competing breweries even sent skilled men to assure that the all-important order was filled. It was, and soldiers would remember the gift as a kindness before Dunkirk and the Blitz and the meat grinders of bloody battles to come.

During the war years, Guinness sales plummeted and Guinness workers suffered. The Park Royal plant was bombed more than once during the German blitz and in October 1940, the ice plant there was completely destroyed; four workers lost their lives. In time, the deaths reached even into the Guinness family itself. Rupert's son, Arthur, had begun the war as a major in the Suffolk Yeomanry. His father's hopes rested upon him: he was the heir apparent to the chairmanship of the family business and the Guinness in line to assume the title of Earl of Iveagh. Arthur certainly proved himself in uniform. He entered Europe behind the initial Allied advance on D-Day and by February of 1945 found himself embroiled in fierce fighting as part of the 218th Battery of the 55th Anti-Tank Regiment. He was killed on February 8 during the battle at Nijmegen in the Netherlands. He was thirty-two and his father grieved him until the end of his days.

Arthur was not the only Guinness to lose his life in the service of country. Rupert's younger brother was Walter Guinness, who bore the title Baron Moyne. He was an experienced, engaging man, a confidant of many a powerful figure, including Prime Minister Churchill. He had served in the House of Commons and then later in the House of Lords. He had also fought in World War I—ironically in the same unit in which Arthur Guinness, his nephew, died during World War II—and he was Churchill's minister of state in Egypt during the threatening time when Hitler's Afrika Korps was but a few desert miles away. In this role, it was Walter's misfortune to be a symbol of England's restrictive policy on Jewish immigration to Palestine, which caused many an advocate for the State of Israel to regard him as an enemy. On November 6, 1944, while returning from the British Embassy in Cairo to his residence on Gezira Island, Walter Guinness—now Lord Moyne—was assassinated by members of the Palmach, a Jewish guerrilla organization.

Churchill was so moved by the death of his friend that he did not trust himself to speak of it on the floor of Parliament for eleven days. When he did, he said, "If our dreams of Zionism are to end in the smoke of the assassins' guns and our labours for its future to produce only a new set of gangsters worthy of Nazi Germany," then England would "have to reconsider the position we have maintained so consistently and so long." In Israel, the Jewish community was stunned. The influential *Haaretz* newspaper said simply, "No more grievous blow has been struck to our cause." If the hardening of British attitudes toward Israel in the years prior to its independence in 1948 were partially a result of this assassination, as many suspected, then *Haaretz* was more correct in this assessment than its readers at the time could have known.

Like his father before him, Rupert Guinness led his company through trusted and skilled men. For years, and in particular during the war years, Guinness's managing director was Ben Newbold, the gifted strategist who had convinced the company to advertise and then had guided this new venture to historic success. Yet in 1946, just after war's end, Newbold died suddenly. It was a tragic loss, for Newbold had led and counseled Guinness through many prosperous decades. Fortunately, just the year before, Rupert had asked yet another gifted man to assist the aging Newbold. His name was Hugh Beaver, a known administrative genius who had done such a fine job as director general and controller general of the Ministry of Works during the war that he was knighted in 1943. With Newbold's death, Beaver took the lead as managing director and began to position Guinness for unprecedented expansion. He was the first nonbrewer to fill the role, but he knew the St. James's Gate and Park Royal facilities well, he respected the family and the heritage, and, as important, he understood the times.

Beaver began to remake the company to accommodate the needs of a new business age. He separated the breweries at St. James's Gate and Park Royal into two freestanding corporate entities under the broader Arthur Guinness, Son & Co. Ltd. umbrella. He respected the science of brewing and so invested huge sums into the continuous sterilization process that Alan McMullen had developed. He also upgraded the fleet of locomotives serving the St. James's Gate facility and purchased new ships in anticipation of broader global markets to come.

Sir Hugh had reason to expect rapid growth. In 1945, Guinness topped two million casks of beer for the first time since 1921. The American market was recovering from a three-decade slump—brought on in large part by Prohibition—and though wartime restrictions and shortages still plagued brewers, there was every reason to believe these would clear in time and great opportunities would await those who were prepared. Beaver intended to be one of them.

To make these hopes reality, Guinness again put its faith in the work of John Gilroy. The trademark Guinness advertisements had offered much encouragement to civilians at home and to soldiers abroad during the war years. Now, Gilroy's seals and toucans, zookeepers, and ostriches returned to peacetime work. By the early 1950s, the famed menagerie leapt from Gilroy's posters into keepsakes that ranged from ceramic images of Guinness animals to table lamps. The popularity of Gilroy's work proved that the advertising campaign had lost none of its luster in the years after the war. So beloved were these symbols of both Guinness and British life that on September 22, 1955, Gilroy's creations starred in the first night of commercial television in British history. Delighted viewers that night watched commercials featuring a live sea lion, a real zoo-keeper, and other puppets and animated characters depicting the familiar Guinness gang. It was confirmation that Guinness the beer and Guinness the family of symbols meant as much to viewers in the United Kingdom as ever.

Yet Guinness had no intention of resting on its advertising laurels, even if they were the creation of a genius like John Gilroy. Other geniuses shaped the company as well and one of them was Arthur Fawcett. He had come to Guinness when the company acquired Alexander MacFee bottling company in 1932. Fawcett had headed that company and then, with its acquisition by Guinness, took charge of Guinness Exports Limited. He was known as "an abrasive personality with imaginative promotional ideas." It was an understatement. Fawcett conceived some of the most brilliant promotional schemes in Guinness history. In the early 1950s, he hit on the idea of distributing thousands of miniature bottles of Guinness stout. These became immensely popular, dramatically increased Guinness brand recognition, and made the three-inch-tall bottles a feature in collections around the world.

In 1954 and 1959, Fawcett executed a scheme that was one of the most unusual and effective in advertising history. He decided Guinness should put messages in thousands of numbered and sealed bottles and drop them in the Atlantic, Indian, and Pacific oceans. The intent was that people would find the bottles and then contact Guinness. "We will most certainly write you back telling you exactly when and where your particular bottle was dropped," the message in the bottle assured, "sending also a suitable memento of the occasion. But, irrespective of anything else, please don't forget the important message that has come to you o'er thousands of miles: Guinness is Good for You!" Fawcett had 50,000 bottles dropped in 1954 and then, as the plan met with success, dropped more than 150,000 in 1959 on Guinness's two-hundredth anniversary.

Fawcett had fulfilled one of the great principles of advertising: don't just sell your product—sell your product's culture. The bottle drop scheme tied the Guinness image to excitement, exploration, discovery, and generosity. Letters began to arrive within months of the first drop, first from as far away as the Azores and then from South America, the West Indies, the Philippines, and India. An explorer even found two bottles in the Arctic Ocean along a beach at Coates Island. The attention the bottle drops drew was unparalleled. The scheme has been called "the world's longest running advertising promotion" and it is likely true. Bottles are still found today at a rate of one or two a year; the fascinating array of letters and responses sent in from all over the world can be seen at the Storehouse at St. James's Gate.

The bottle drops were indicative of the experimentation and innovation that marked Hugh Beaver's era at Guinness. So was the book he conceived, which also boasts the Guinness name—the book that has surely launched a billion wagers. It came about on a hunting trip in County Wexford in 1951. Sir Hugh and a friend began a gentle argument about the fastest game bird in England; was it the golden plover or the grouse? But they could find no book that would solve the matter, not at their hunting lodge or at the bookstores in town. Beaver began to see the virtues of a book that would contain every type of statistic that might arise in discussions at pubs and sports clubs.

He mentioned the book at the Guinness offices and an aide suggested the names of two men who ran a fact-checking service in London. They might be just the ones to create such a book, he was told. The two men were Norris and Ross McWhirter, twins in their mid-twenties who worked as sports writers. Beaver met them, hired them, and put them to work. He intended the book only as a promotional gimmick for pubs in Ireland and the United Kingdom. In fact, his plan was to simply give the book away, trusting that Guinness would recoup its costs in sales of beer.

It was called *The Guinness Book of Records*. Published merely as a handout in 1954, the next year it topped the British best-seller lists. No one was more surprised than Sir Hugh. When it was published in the United States in 1956, it sold more than seventy thousand copies. It has since become one of the best-selling books in history, with hundreds of millions sold in more than one hundred countries. Perhaps as important, it has carried the Guinness name to nations and to generations that did not know that name from the reputation of the legendary beer alone.

If it is the job of a managing director to create an environment in which vision and innovation thrive, then Sir Hugh Beaver was certainly doing his job in the 1950s. In addition to creative advertising campaigns, best-selling books, and administrative reorganizations, Sir Hugh also called for a more inventive approach to serving the beloved black stout. Though Guinness profits rose in this decade, challengers were at the door. Lager intruded into many markets and planners at the company began realizing that they needed some way to make their stout more attractive. They settled on changing how Guinness was served, how its consistency was maintained, and how it was presented to the customer.

Traditionally, a Guinness was poured at a pub from a cask that sat high above the bar and also from one that rested below. This was how the beer and the carbonation needed to give that beer life were merged in the customer's glass. Too many moving parts, though, allowed opportunity for the system to malfunction. Also, too much was left up to the bartender. The balance of carbonation and beer might not be right. Or, if the beer was too cold, it was flat; if it was too warm, it was too frothy. Guinness wanted to solve these problems to win a broader market share—with a beer that was consistently good wherever it was served.

Sir Hugh put the development of a solution into the hands of a young engineer named Michael Ash. Within the company, Ash's project, officially named the Draught Project, was snickered at as the "Daft Project." Few believed it would be a success. Yet in 1958, Ash presented Sir Hugh with a system he had christened "Easy Serve." It was a system based on a single metal cask that combined two sections—one for the stout and the other containing the right pressurized mixture of carbon dioxide and nitrogen. It was revolutionary but it wasn't enough; the Guinness brewers weren't quite happy with it. Ash sensed that he had taken a step in the right direction but that there was a better invention to come.

In time, Ash's innovation would lead to a single-part keg in which the carbon dioxide and nitrogen were already infused into the stout. It would change beer delivery forever, but not so much as a later development that would spring from it. It's worth jumping ahead in our story to see how Michael Ash's half step led to one of the great innovations in the delivery of beer.

In the early 1980s, when canning beer had become popular, the challenge for Guinness was to make sure its beer was delivered with consistent taste—yet also with its famed creamy head. Guinness engineers were set to the task and a variety of solutions were offered. All were found wanting. Finally, in 1985, engineers developed the In-Can System (ICS). This was an ingenious plastic disk that was inserted at the bottom of a 500-milliliter can. To state it simply, the disk, which was later called a widget (and is, in its current incarnation, a floating sphere), would release nitrogen when the can was opened, thus allowing the creamy head characteristic of Guinness to emerge.

The widget was so advanced and inspired that in 1991 it won the Queen's Award for Technological Achievement. In 2003, the British people voted it the greatest invention in forty years. Now, many brewers have copied the technology and use some form of the widget, but it all began with young Michael Ash in the 1950s—and with the culture of innovation that Sir Hugh Beaver encouraged at St. James's Gate.

There was more to come. It had not escaped the Guinness board's notice that lager beer was becoming the most popular type of beer in the world. It was perceived as a threat, for

Photo by Isaac Darnall

Fermentation chambers at the Guinness Storehouse

lager is far different from stout. Lager, which comes from a German word meaning "to store," is brewed with a different type of yeast than stout—a "bottom-fermenting" *Saccharomyces carlsbergensis* rather than a "top-fermenting" *Saccharomyces cerevisiae*—and it is kept dramatically colder than stout. The result is a golden-colored beer that is lighter and less bitter and allows for greater variety of flavors than stout. This likely explains its great popularity everywhere but in England and Ireland during the twentieth century.

To answer this rising market for lager, Guinness decided during 1959 to create its own lager. For at least a few older heads at Guinness, the move must have reminded them of a lesson from an earlier day. Just after World War II, Guinness had tried to make the former Burke Brewery in Long Island a profitable venture. After heavy investment, an American-made Guinness Extra Stout was released in March 1948. Sadly, the Long Island venture would last barely six years. Heavy competition and Guinness's inexperience in the American market took their toll. Many concluded, as one American commentator put it, "You can't sell black beer in a blond market." Now, in 1960, Guinness would sell blond beer, reversing the decision of its founder, Arthur Guinness, to sell only stout. Called Harp Lager, after the famous Brian Boru harp that had for so long been the Guinness symbol, the Guinness lager would prove a major success and continue as a treasured product for decades to come.

Harp was perhaps the last of many innovations during Rupert Guinness's chairmanship of the company. By 1962, he was eighty-eight years old and it was time, so family members said, to pass control to a new generation. It is a moment we should mark carefully. The heir apparent was Arthur Francis Benjamin, known simply as Benjamin, who was only twenty-five. He had no brewery experience and he had not chosen a brewer's life as his own. It is perhaps best to cite Michele Guinness's insightful description of this historic change.

> Shy and retiring, finding public occasions something of a strain, Benjamin was the epitome of a man who had greatness thrust upon him. When the first Arthur Guinness' eldest son decided to become a clergyman, the second Arthur had taken his place. When the second Arthur's eldest son became a clergyman and the second son a poet, Benjamin Lee stepped into the gap. When Benjamin Lee's eldest son, Lord Ardilaun, resigned from the partnership, Edward Cecil was more than able to take over. Edward Cecil had three sons, two of whom made exceptional contributions to the firm. He also drew in his wife's family. So the descent from father to son had been preserved for five generations and two hundred years. Benjamin Iveagh had no say in his destiny. He could not choose to be a clergyman or a poet, a doctor or a postman for that matter. The buck stopped with him.

It was a change, then, but not just in the tone of the transition. It was a change from a generation that embodied the historic Guinness values. Benjamin, the new head of the firm, was a fine man and there would be many advances during his more than two decades at the helm. Guinness would begin to be brewed in Africa and Malaysia and would expand its markets beyond anything known before. The company would diversify into fields such as publishing and movies, restaurants and real estate, trucking, and even confections. It would also expand into a field that many a Guinness ancestor would have opposed: distilled spirits. First acquiring Arthur Bell & Sons, a distiller of premium whiskey, Guinness would go on to purchase other such firms and gain a reputation as a purveyor of alcohol in all its drinkable forms, rather than just a brewer of beer. It was a historic shift and one that would ultimately lead the company into mergers that meant its demise as an independent firm.

The passing of the baton from Rupert to Benjamin signaled the end of an era of Guinness tradition. The men who had owned the company and then later chaired the board were men who drew their values from a deep family well. They knew how to brew beer, yes, but they also knew how to care for their employees, how to invest wealth for social good, and how to create corporate cultures that would change the course of nations. It was Rupert, after all—the one the family never expected to come to much—who took his £5 million wedding gift from his father and then went to live in the slums, becoming an advocate for the poor and downtrodden in a manner befitting his fam-

The Guinness Storehouse today

ily heritage. He was an exceptional man, one shaped by compassion and adversity, and the legacy that he embodied did not die with the transition to Benjamin . . . but it did weaken and begin to fade.

In 1986, when Benjamin was not yet fifty, he decided to stand down from the chairmanship and to accept the title of president. The chairmanship thus passed from family hands for the first time in Guinness history. The truth was that Guinness had simply outgrown the Guinnesses. The acquisitions and the diversification had all made it too much. The rate of growth was beyond belief, almost beyond comprehension. In 1983, Guinness's net assets were £250 million. Just four years later that number had quadrupled to more than £1 billion. Guinness had become one of the most powerful corporations in the world and the responsibilities of the chairman were too much for someone who had merely inherited it without having chosen it as a life's call.

The Guinness firm would continue to rise even after the Guinness family stepped from prominence. There would be scandals, of course, like the one that placed Ernest Saunders—Benjamin Guinness's successor—in jail. And there would always be challenges, like the eventual recognition that Guinness had overreached in all of its diversification and needed to simplify. And always there would be the wonderful advertisements, like the wildly popular "Genius" ads, or the "The Man with the Guinness" commercials starring the ruggedly handsome Rutger Hauer,

Photo by Isaac Darnall

or even the delightful "Brilliant!" ads of later years. And then, of course, there was the dramatic merger with Grand Metropolitan in 1997 to create Diageo, the largest alcohol beverage company in the world. Now Diageo continues to extend the Guinness brand, taking it to new shores and new generations with each passing year.

We should be thankful that they do. We should be grateful there is a magnificent Storehouse in Dublin that explains the genius of Guinness and keeps something of the heritage alive. Still, it is not Diageo's job to extend the more spiritual version of that Guinness heritage. It is not their responsibility to speak of the faith of Arthur or the compassion of Edward Cecil and Dr. Lumsden or the self-sacrifice of Rupert and the Grattan line. No, that part of the heritage will only live when men absorb it from the Guinness story and embed it in fertile fields of their own.

EPILOGUE:
THE GUINNESS WAY

The walk from the Guinness brewery at St. James's Gate to Trinity College Dublin requires only fifteen minutes. It is one of the loveliest walks in Europe. A man turns down one of the many northbound lanes of the brewery, the smell of malt in his nostrils, and then moves east on Thomas Street. He passes through the Liberties, then, and toward the city center on one of the most famed market streets in Dublin. After but a few steps on High Street, he turns down Dame Street toward the college.

On this historic avenue, named for ancient Dame's Gate that adjoined the Church of St. Mary del Dame, our walker takes in some of the most inviting restaurants that Dublin has to offer. He will pass, too, the Bank of Ireland, the City Hall, and the side street leading to Dublin Castle, before approaching the gates to Trinity College. He cannot enter without passing the statue of Henry Grattan, the eighteenth-century Irish statesman who once wrote that brewing was "the natural nurse of the people and entitled to every encouragement, favor and exemption." Guinnesses passing his statue must surely have tipped their hats to this patron time and again.

Then, of course, there is Trinity College itself. It is a

Photo by Isaac Darnall

Looking up Dame Street from Trinity College, with the statue of Henry Grattan and the Bank of Ireland (with columns) on the right

grand example of an Elizabethan university staking her claim to greatness in the modern world. Its forty-seven acres are adorned with cobblestone streets and buildings that have stood where they are for nearly five hundred years. But then there are the modern structures, shiny and high-tech, which prove that this is no sleepy, backward-looking institution.

If we could make this fifteen-minute walk and travel not only a few miles but a few hundred years, we would find that one of the most treasured fields of study at Trinity was a topic we do not teach today, one that we have neglected to our own harm. It was called moral philosophy and it was a blend of history, theology, philosophy, and ethics. It was, in short, history writ large, a look at the past to gain the lessons that might be learned. Men studied history in this manner primarily to discern the ways of Providence and so acquire wisdom for their own age. Far from the ivory tower, abstracted-from-reality approach so prevalent in our modern universities, the study of earlier ages was then considered eminently practical and men expected to live differently for the time they spent in the far-off country of the past.

It seems appropriate that this is the approach we should take to the Guinness story. Now that we have followed the broad outlines of this family's journey through two and a half centuries of history, it seems that the story demands a moral philosophy approach, one like that which would have been taken at Trinity College all those centuries ago.

Photo by Isaac Darnall

Trinity College Dublin, established in 1592 by Queen Elizabeth I, is Ireland's oldest university. Rupert Guinness made several important donations to Trinity. Pictured here is the Graduate Memorial Building

What might we learn from the Guinness tale that we can emulate? What are the pillars of truth we can make our own? What are the distilled maxims of the Guinness experience that can lift us, too, beyond what we have known?

Let us consider the Guinness Way.

1. Discern the ways of God for life and business.

Harry Grattan Guinness had a favorite saying, one that he had borrowed from the wisdom of Prince Albert: "Gentlemen, find out the will of God for your day and generation, and then, as quickly as possible, get into line."

There is little question that much of the Guinness success and much of the Guinness impact on society came from living in light of this maxim of conduct. It began with a man's individual life. It is not hard to imagine the first Arthur Guinness wondering, as we all do, about what his role in this life might be. He would consider his abilities, ponder what he sensed while in church, mull over what men like his father and his godfather the archbishop might have said about his future, and think deeply about what brought him pride and joy. In time, he would recognize his skills as a brewer and make it his life's work.

But there would be more. He would also wonder what God's will for his life might be, beyond the brewing and the redemptive use of wealth. Why was he born in his time with its unique configuration of blessings and plagues? And he would come to see what God was doing, how answering poverty and lifting men through a knowledge of God's word and striving to end the bloody vanity of duels would all be the work his Savior might be about. And so he threw himself into these tasks. He started Sunday schools and gave generously to the poor and took a stand again the bloodshed that tainted his age.

In all this, he was a success, and not just him alone but those who came after. We know from his own words that the second Arthur asked these questions of his life and even those who followed him and who were not as passionate about their faith nevertheless tried to understand their lives in terms of a purpose God might be fulfilling in their time. So this hope to know God's will and fulfill it became a motive force in the Guinness line and it points a way to success for us as well.

2. Think in terms of generations yet to come.

Historians tell us that more than twenty-three generations were required to complete the glorious Canterbury Cathedral of England. We know that men sometimes worked all their lives on a portico or a vault or a series of pillars, understanding their labors as an offering to God. And when they were about to die, they often asked to be taken to the place they had worked in the cathedral. With their family gathered around them, they would pass their tools to their sons and commend the next generation to further progress on that tabernacle of God. Then, in peace, they would pass from this life.

It is a vision that is easily lost, this idea of each generation playing a role in a larger purpose, but it has proven a pathway to success time and again. It is also part of the wisdom of the Guinness saga. Looking back over the centuries at St. James's Gate, we can see the sons of wealthy men working beside day-wage laborers, learning the skills of brewing until they became the best they could be. Some of the Guinness men apprenticed for more years than they were allowed to lead, but this learning at the side of older men was always understood as the path to power.

It is a lesson we ought to absorb and apply to our own work. We tend to think short term. We tend to expect each generation to start from the beginning and then rise on its own. But this is a modern way of thinking. In ages past, each generation was expected to launch the next, and great families of wealth and influence arose as a result. Perhaps this can be the meaning of Guinness for us, that we learn again to build for centuries rather than decades and that we do so selflessly, knowing that the measure of our lives is not determined at our death but rather in the lives and accomplishments of generations yet to come.

3. Whatever else you do, do at least one thing very well.

When Rupert Guinness served in the House of Lords, he hardly ever rose to speak. In fact, we know the exact words of the only speech he ever made. It seems that one day a fellow member, a peer, was complaining about all the signs he saw in the beautiful British countryside that boasted "Guinness is good for you." After this went on for some time, the man ended his tirade. Finally, the nearly ninety-year-old Rupert rose and gave a memorable speech comprised of five simple words: "Guinness *is* good for you!" the eminent Lord Iveagh shouted. It was the shortest but perhaps among the most heartfelt speeches in the history of that venerable institution.

Beer was what Rupert Guinness knew. Beer was what the Guinness fortune had been made from and beer was what the heads of the brewery ever labored to better produce. Yes, there were other interests among the Guinnesses and, yes, there were other pursuits, but for the brewing

Guinnesses, making beer was the guiding passion of their business lives.

It would be the folly of later generations to spread themselves too thin and to overdiversify until they nearly lost the excellence of their founding task. But in the early days, in the days that made the fortune and the brand, it was doing one thing well and linking all other pursuits to it that made Guinness among the greatest names in the world.

It is a lesson we might reclaim today. There is certainly a place for diversification, but it should be attempted only after a solid base is built and only if that solid base is comprised of the one thing the man or the corporation does well. Then, if that foundation is broad enough and strong enough, perhaps it can support a number of pursuits. Yet always the one thing must come first and always the passion for excellence at that one thing must be nurtured. This is a Guinness key to success.

4. Master the facts before you act.

There is a wonderful quote from a time when the Guinness company was making a major decision about breaking into new markets. In an explanation of the company's thinking, a manager wrote, "We followed our traditional policy of considering long and acting quickly."

It was the Guinness way. Once the facts were in and the data processed, once the context was understood and all variations considered, then action was taken and taken decisively. But only then. First, myths had to be exploded, lazy thinking exposed. Junior men had to be sent back for more research and the conventional wisdom challenged until it proved itself. It was an approach that undid impatient men, but the heads at Guinness didn't care. Impatient men hadn't built fortunes and brewed history-making beer. Impatient men were driven to mistakes by their eagerness to simply move on. No, impatient men had to be tempered, checked, and chastised, while wise men held off decisions until the knowledge they needed was complete.

It is an approach that would serve us well today, when data passes itself off as information and speed is offered as a substitute to wise planning and strategies well designed. In an age in which knowledge increases nearly exponentially, it is easy to become lazy and move too fast. No, the wise man today, like the wise man in the first Arthur's day, defies pressure in order to ponder and even to pray. And then he acts, when he knows who he is and what he should do, when he has anticipated the results and when his resources are rightly prepared. This is the decision making that leads to fortune and it may take greater courage than any other task a good leader must fulfill.

5. Invest in those you would have invest in you.
Edward Cecil, the wise business head who took Guinness to new heights, once said, "You cannot make money from people unless you are willing for people to make money from you."

This is nearly a reversal of business thinking today. The goal today seems to be to squeeze the worker until he can give no more. Rather than invest in him, rather than seek his good so he is better able to seek the good of his employer, we instead set up a tension between labor and management that is counterproductive to both.

We seem to have forgotten the idea of a corporate destiny—that workers and owners, labor and management, prosper together or decline separately. We have forgotten that in a moral free market, social uplift best happens through the power of benevolent employment. It is in the world of work that men gain skills, have character modeled for them, gain a broader education, learn to lead, and are given the tools of advancements for their families.

Guinness understood this. The company did not drain a man and then expect the church or the state to rebuild him again. They invested. They paid high wages, offered every type of education, provided medicine, sports, entertainment, and even a place to think, and assured every kind of financial safety net for those who served them well. They also built houses, sent sons to college, and lifted whole families to new economic heights. They did this because it was the right thing to do, yes, but also because it made their firm more successful than those who did not understand this vital kind of investment.

The truth is as Edward Cecil proclaimed: we must invest in those who serve us if we expect them to serve well. It is one of the great pillars of the Guinness legacy and it is wisdom that we should reclaim, particularly in our modern economic world of tension and strife.

These, then, are but a few of the maxims from the Guinness experience that promise to help us do well. They are the distilled truths of two and a half centuries of experience and the proven wisdom of one of the world's great brands. And we, having read a bit of their story and pondered their meaning in time, would do well to learn their moral philosophy and to apply it to great, moral ventures of our own.

ACKNOWLEDGMENTS

As a visitor to the world of brewing and beer, I initially needed as much help with the Guinness story as I might have had I been writing about the planet Mars. Thankfully, I had good people to help me, men and women of faith and poetry and skill.

It was Dr. George Grant who first introduced me to the idea that beer has a noble history and that great saints of old loved it, drank it, wrote about it, and celebrated it to the glory of God. I am grateful to him for this as I am for so many things, including that he tolerates my many demands for his time.

I spent a fascinating morning at Blackstone's Restaurant and Brewery in Nashville learning about brewing firsthand. Owner Stephanie Weins made me welcome, and Travis

Hixon and Josh Garrett taught this novice much of what I needed to know about malt and wort and gravity and yeast. I absorbed their love of brewing just as I came to respect their skill and I am grateful for my hours in their world. Bobby Blazier made this connection for me, as he has so many others, and I love him for his passion for all things, including beer.

Master Brewer Rob Higginbotham patiently spent hours teaching me his trade and since he is a poet as well as a craftsman, he gave me ways to lovingly communicate the art of beer I would never have otherwise known. I am grateful.

A writer does his work as he holds the world at bay and then, when he is done, he reverses himself and yearns for affirmation and praise. Those who mix praise with loving criticism do him the most good, though, and I have had more than my fair share of friends skilled at this art. Jeff Pack, my raucous and loving fellow writer, gave wise counsel, as did Isaac Darnall, who not only offered a journalist's feedback about what I have written but traveled to Ireland with me to take many of the marvelous photographs found in this book. His artistry and his teasing insistence that I love beer as he does have made my work better than it would have been.

Joel Miller, my friend and publisher at Thomas Nelson, has a love for beer and beer history that exceeds my own. He has given sage advice and tender encouragement when it was needed most. I am, once again, grateful.

The good people of Guinness at St. James's Gate in

Dublin could not have a better archivist than Eibhlin Roche. She is articulate, learned, a master of resources, and a fascinating person to interview. I'm grateful for the hours I spent in her archives and the wisdom she offered for my work.

It has been one of the great honors of my life to have a member of the Guinness family care about this book. Michele Guinness—whose own *The Genius of Guinness* is a masterpiece—has both instructed and encouraged. Her kindness and passion for the Grattan story is an inspiration.

Finally, if a man finds a loving wife in this life, he finds a good thing. If he finds in that same wife a friend, he is twice blessed. But if he finds as well a skilled partner who builds with him professionally while at all times being that lover and friend, he should fall to his knees often and thank God that there is mercy for the undeserving. I do, often, for I have Beverly—and I am grateful beyond words.

BIBLIOGRAPHY

I have great admiration for those who write about Guinness. It is not for the faint of heart. The Guinness family members themselves seldom participate, there have been lawsuits against writers who offended, and literary disagreements have been known to descend into personal vendettas and vicious betrayals. Then there is the scope of the story. The Guinness tale can range from the theme of a Beatles song—"A Day in the Life" was likely written about the death of a Guinness heir—to the preaching of John Wesley, from poverty in nineteenth-century Dublin to strictures against alcohol in modern Dubai.

I have escaped most of these dangers because my purpose has been simply to describe the faith and generosity of Guinness. Details of brewing, controversies over genealogies, and gossip about the Guinness elite I have left to others. I trust I am on safe ground.

Loving the Guinness story as I do, it is my hope that someone will do for Guinness the family what Diageo has done for Guinness the company: develop an archive. There is no depository of Guinness family documents, no research center or museum honoring the nobility of Arthur Guinness's descendants. This is unfortunate, for theirs is too grand a story to leave to cartons of documents abandoned in attics. We should hope that a new generation of Guinnesses will address this need, for they will be serving well both their heirs and their fellow man if they do.

*　　*　　*

I should describe some of the resources I have used. In the **Introduction**, the information about Guinness's benevolence with its employees comes from a fascinating little booklet titled *Guide to St. James's Brewery*. It was published by Arthur Guinness, Son & Co. Ltd. in 1928 and is the best snapshot of that era of Guinness history I have found. It is barely one hundred pages including photographs, but it is so interesting and inspiring I would be thrilled to see a version of it sold at the Storehouse today.

The information on the Pilgrims and beer at the beginning of **Before There Was Guinness** is from William Bradford's *Of Plymouth Plantation, 1620–1647* and *Mourt's Relation*, our two primary sources for the Pilgrim experience in the New World. For the story of beer in the ancient and medieval world, Gregg Smith's *Beer: A History of Suds and Civilization from Mesopotamia to Microbreweries* and Tom Standage's *A History of the World in 6 Glasses* were both enjoyable and essential. For the later history of beer leading up to the rise of Guinness, particularly the history of beer in the Christian church, *Drinking with Calvin and Luther: A History of Alcohol in the Church* by Jim West and *God Gave Wine: What the Bible Says About Alcohol* by Kenneth L. Gentry Jr. were learned guides.

The fascinating thesis of Dr. Solomon H. Katz is summarized best in a *New York Times* article of March 4, 1987. It is titled "Does Civilization Owe a Debt to Beer?" and is widely available on the Internet, as are discussions of Dr. Katz's fascinating work as an anthropologist at the University of Pennsylvania.

Bill Yenne's *Guinness: The 250-year Quest for the Perfect Pint*, which provided valuable information on the history of beer for this first chapter, is, I believe, the best book on Guinness the beer. Though his work is helpful as a corporate history, Yenne is at his best when he is describing matters like the evolution of brewing, the life of yeast, or Guinness's contributions to brewing science. His writing is that of a journalist and his straightforward reportage makes this the best popular textbook on Guinness brewing.

In writing **The Rise of Arthur,** I found Patrick Guinness's *Arthur's Round: The Life and Times of Brewing Legend*

Arthur Guinness to be encyclopedic and wonderfully contentious. The author was eager to expose some of the myths that have surrounded his forebear and also did Guinness historians a great service with his vast knowledge of Arthur's Ireland. That he takes on other Guinness historians by name and that he is willing to spend pages on background and context make this book a technical but sometimes surprisingly poetic read.

The most beautifully written of all Guinness books is Michele Guinness's *The Genius of Guinness*. Though her work focuses primarily on the Grattan line of Guinnesses for God, she provides insights into the brewery Guinnesses that are wise and instructive.

My chapter **At the Same Place By Their Ancestors** was well served by Yenne and Michele Guinness, but also by *The Silver Salver: The Story of the Guinness Family* by Frederic Mullally. Though his focus is more on the lives of Guinness luminaries than brewing lore or faith, Mullally captures much of the modern tale of the Guinness clan that most other Guinness books neglect. A similar book is *Dark and Light: The Story of the Guinness Family* by Derek Wilson. I found Wilson's work to be among the most helpful in understanding the historical context of Guinness. I also admire Wilson for doing justice to the religious influences in Guinness history, something that many historians neglect or treat merely as a curiosity.

For my chapter **The Good That Wealth Can Do**, I relied on both Tony Corcoran's *The Goodness of Guinness: The*

Brewery, Its People and the City of Dublin and Corcoran's monograph on the same topic in the Storehouse Archives. This author has served us well with his celebration of Guinness benevolence, his exploration of Dr. Lumsden's work, and his delightful portrayal of Guinness goodness in his own family line and childhood.

I found the writings of Dr. Charles Cameron to be very helpful and, thankfully, many of his reports are widely available on the Internet. For the background of Dr. Lumsden's work and for a portrait of Dublin's poor in the latter part of the nineteenth century, Cameron's writings are essential.

I drew from Michele Guinness's *The Genius of Guinness* for much of what I have written in **The Guinnesses for God.** In my conversations with her, I learned that she has many of Henry Grattan Guinness's letters and books in her possession and that this has enabled her to write as movingly as she has of this great man's life. The world still awaits a major biography of this important Christian leader and I hope Michele Guinness will find a way to take on this task. His writings alone warrant the attention, not to mention his leadership of one of the most transforming religious revivals in Irish history.

For **Twentieth-Century Guinness,** Bill Yenne was the most helpful, though a quirky little book called *Guinness is Guinness . . . The Colorful Story of a Black and White Brand* by Mark Griffiths provided rich details and a needed laugh. Crude and partisan, learned and lighthearted, Griffiths's work is the most accessible on modern Guinness, Diageo, and the brilliant advertising that makes Guinness an icon in popular culture. I also found Michele Guinness's depiction of Rupert Guinness tender and beautiful and was inspired by her hopes for Guinness generations yet to come.

Though I have relied heavily on the books I have mentioned, I have also found the following to be valuable. *Guinness 1886–1939: From Incorporation to the Second World War* by S. R. Dennison and Oliver MacDonagh is essentially a corporate report but with moments of reflection and beauty. *A Bottle of Guinness Please: The Colourful History of Guinness* by David Hughes is a highly technical but richly illustrated and lovingly written book that no student of Guinness history should fail to consult. Finally, Jonathan Guinness's *Requiem for a Family Business* may be about the scandals of the 1980s but it provides a reflection—indeed, almost a lament—on the meaning of Guinness history that is unlike anything else in print.

ABOUT THE AUTHOR

Stephen Mansfield is the *New York Times* best-selling author of more than a dozen books on history, biography, and contemporary culture. He founded and heads the Mansfield Group (Mansfieldgroup.com), a consulting and communications firm, and has also founded Chartwell Literary Group (Chartwellliterary.com), a highly successful company that creates and manages literary projects.

Mansfield grew up the son of a United States Army officer and as a result spent the majority of his youth in Europe. Returning to the United States to attend college, he earned a bachelor's degree in history and theology. He later earned a master's degree in history and public policy and a doctorate in history and literature.

He began his writing career with a book on Winston Churchill titled *Never Give In,* which became a Gold Medallion Award Finalist. He then wrote biographies of Booker T. Washington and George Whitefield. In 1997, the governor of Tennessee commissioned him to write the official history of religion in Tennessee for that state's bicentennial.

In 2003, Mansfield wrote his groundbreaking work, *The Faith of George W. Bush,* which spent many weeks on the *New York Times* best-seller list and was credited with shaping the national dialogue about religion in American politics. He followed up this book with a study of faith among American soldiers in Iraq titled *The Faith of the American Soldier* and with a book on Pope Benedict XVI, which *Publisher's Weekly* called "an inviting study of a new world leader."

In 2008, Mansfield wrote *The Faith of Barack Obama,* which was intended as an objective look at the nontraditional religious life of the nation's first African American president. The book was highly controversial because the author—who is a theological and political conservative—insisted on a tone of impartiality and kindness in writing about a man with whom he disagreed. This book was a best seller and was credited with capturing well the religious themes at play in the 2008 presidential election.

Beyond his influential writing career, Mansfield is a popular speaker on themes of faith, heritage, achievement, and leadership. He has also worked both in the United States and abroad on issues of poverty and social justice. He lives primarily in Nashville, Tennessee, with his beloved wife, Beverly, who is a successful songwriter and producer.